The Theology of Change

THE THEOLOGY
OF CHANGE

A CHRISTIAN CONCEPT OF GOD
IN AN EASTERN PERSPECTIVE

Jung Young Lee

ORBIS BOOKS
Maryknoll, New York 10545

"Diagram of Cosmic Evolution in Terms of the Sixty-four Hexagrams," and "Circular Diagram of the Sixty-four Hexagrams," in *The Period of Classical Learning*, Vol II of Fung Yu-Lan, *A History of Chinese Philosophy*, transl. by Derk Bodde, pp. 459 and 462. Reprinted by permission of Princeton University Press.

Library of Congress Cataloging in Publication Data

Lee, Jung Young.
   The theology of change.

   Includes bibliographical references.
    1. God—Addresses, essays, lectures. 2. Theology, Doctrinal—Addresses, essays, lectures. 3. Process theology—Addresses, essays, lectures. I. Title.
ISBN 0-88344-492-5

The Catholic Foreign Mission Society of America (Maryknoll) recruits and trains people for overseas missionary service. Through Orbis Books Maryknoll aims to foster the international dialogue that is essential to mission. The books published, however, reflect the opinions of their authors and are not meant to represent the official position of the Society.

To
J. ROBERT NELSON,
my teacher, colleague, and friend

CONTENTS

Acknowledgments   ix

Introduction   1
The *I Ching* and Its Metaphysical System   1
The *Yin* and *Yang* Principles   3
Duograms and Trigrams   5
Hexagrams   7

Chapter I
Theology of Change: The Quest of Its Methodology   11
Orientations of Traditional Theology   11
Process Theology and Theology of Change   13
The Theology of Change as Valid Theology   20

Chapter II
Change as Ultimate Reality: God as Change Itself   29
The Nonsymbolic Nature of God in Judeo-Christian Tradition   30
The Nonsymbolic Nature of God in Eastern Traditions   32
The Nonsymbolic Nature of God as "Is-ness" Itself   35
The Dynamics of God's "Is-ness Itself"   36
God as Change-Itself   38
Summary   42
"Change-Itself" as Changeless   43

Chapter III
Both-And as Ultimate Reality: God as Inclusiveness   49
God as Both Personal and Impersonal   50
God as Both Male and Female   50
Problems and Limitations of a Personal God   52
Problems of God and Evil   57

Chapter IV
Change as the Source of Creativity: God as Creator   67
    The Neglected Creator God   67
    Creator-Centered Theology   68
    God as the Source of Creativity   69
    Creator and Creature   73
    Orders of Creative Process   78
    Change as the Creator   80

Chapter V
The Perfect Realization of Change: Jesus Christ   86
    Problems of Christology   88
    Christ as the Word   89
    Christ as the Light   91
    Christ as the Savior   92
    Christ as the Center of the Creative Process   97
    Divinity and Humanity of Christ   98
    The Crucifixion and Resurrection of Christ   100

Chapter VI
The Spirit and the Unity of Change:
The Holy Spirit and the Trinity   103
    The Meaning of Spirit   103
    Spirit and Matter   104
    Spirit as Life and Power   106
    Spirit as Inner Essence   109
    Spirit as *Yin*   110
    Problems of the Trinity   111
    The Trinity in "Both-And" Logic   114

Chapter VII
Further Implications of the Theology of Change   120
    The Freedom of Human Will   121
    Natural Theology in the Christian Faith   122
    The Wrath of God in Theology   124
    God's Passibility   125
    The Resurrection of the Dead   126
    The Idea of *Eschaton*   128

Index   133

ACKNOWLEDGMENTS

In preparing this book I owe a great deal to countless scholars and friends in this country as well as abroad. Even though it is almost impossible to recognize every one of them, I feel I am compelled to mention a few names. I would like to express my gratitude to Professor David Griffin of Claremont School of Theology, Professor James Will of Garrett Evangelical Theological Seminary, and Professor Lewis S. Ford, editor of *Process Studies*, for their communications in regard to my manuscript. I am especially grateful to Professor Lewis S. Ford, who gave me constructive and critical reviews of my methodology in regard to process theology. Most of all, I am most grateful to Professor J. Robert Nelson of Boston University School of Theology, to whom this book is dedicated in his spirit of ecumenicity.

The third chapter is the revision of my original essay, "Can God Be Change Itself?," which was originally published in the *Journal of Ecumenical Studies* (Fall 1973). I am grateful to the Editor of the journal and Temple University for permission to use the article in this book.

I owe my gratitude to Naomi Richard and John Eagleson of Orbis Books, who have done an excellent job in improving style and clarifying meaning. I am also thankful to my student, Steve Axtman, who has carefully prepared the index for this book. Finally, I must not fail to recognize my wife, Gy, and two children, Sue and Jong, whose patience and sacrifices have made it possible for me to complete this book.

JUNG YOUNG LEE

Grand Forks, North Dakota

INTRODUCTION

We are people of universal process and of a world civilization. West and East are no longer separate worlds. Among the topics for thought resulting from that expansion of the ecumene are the new and increasing ecumenism in West and East, the compatibility of Christian faith with the contemporary scientific worldview, and Christian theological sensitivity to the ecosystem. Valid theology must encompass these topics, for our conclusions on these topics will, I think, shape our future religious faith as well as our educational and social structures. In Chapters I through VI I have attempted to explore the Christian concept of God through valid theology. Chapter VII suggests some implications of this theology for other questions concerning Christian faith.

In the past the Christian faith has been almost exclusively conveyed through the medium of Hellenistic thinking. The inability of Christianity to coexist with other religions in Asia can be attributed predominantly to its inseparability from the Hellenistic way of thinking.[1] If Christianity is to be a vital viable faith in world civilization, it must be capable of being expressed and conveyed in many different philosophical modes. The need to express the Christian faith in eastern terms, which are quite different from Hellenistic terms, becomes increasingly urgent. I have attempted to meet this need—to present a Christian concept of God in eastern terms—in these essays.

THE *I CHING* AND ITS METAPHYSICAL SYSTEM

A metaphysical and cosmological system that has molded common assumptions and recondite philosophies in China, Korea, and Japan is found in the *I ching*, or Book of Changes. The metaphysics of the *I ching*, summed up in the *yin-yang* relationship, represents the primordial ethos and thinking of

1

most East Asian peoples. The *I ching* is one of the first, perhaps the oldest, of the Confucian classics.[2] Its place in the orthodox philosophical canon has been unquestioned since the second century B.C. It became the intellectual basis of both Taoism and Neo-Confucianism[3] and the foundation for later developments in divination, geomancy, astronomy, music, medicine, and other arts and sciences. Its influence on the metaphysics and cosmology of East Asia is comparable to the influence of Plato in the West. If, as Whitehead remarked, all western philosophies are only footnotes to Plato, most East Asian philosophies could be called, by analogy, only commentaries on the *I ching.*

Jung called the *I ching* the quintessential expression of the Chinese mind: "This work [the *I ching*] embodies, as perhaps no other, the spirit of Chinese culture, for the best minds of China have collaborated upon it and contributed to it for thousands of years. Despite its fabulous age it has never grown old, but still lives and operates, at least for those who understand its meaning."[4] Jung considered it not only a metaphysical system but also the germinal standard work of Chinese science. When he was asked by the president of the British Anthropological Society to explain why so highly intellectual a people as the Chinese had produced no science, he answered, "This must really be an optical illusion, because the Chinese did have a 'science' whose 'standard work' was the *I ching,* but . . . the principle of this science, like so much else in China, was altogether different from our scientific principle."[5] The current popularity of this book in the West seems to reaffirm the perennial significance of its metaphysics and cosmology. Since *I ching,* or Book of Changes, embodies East Asian scientific and metaphysical principles, I shall use its ideas to reinterpret the Christian concept of God.

Since many people think of *I ching* simply as a manual for divination and augury I shall begin by summarizing its metaphysical principles. As its title indicates, it is the book or classic (*ching*) of change (*i*). Its theme is change, or *i*, which is the ultimate reality of all things. The etymology of the logogram *i* (𝄇) aids in understanding the concept of change. The archaic pictogram ᗧᵢₗ is defined by an old Chinese dictionary as "chameleon."[6] Since the basic characteristic of a chameleon is changeableness (its color changes many times a day), the word *i* was believed to have been adopted to signify change in the *I ching.*

The metaphysical meaning of change, however, can be derived from the composition of the modern logogram (易), which consists of two parts: 日 , which means "sun," and 勿 ,which means "to give up" but is often understood as the old form of 月 , or "moon." In other words, the word *i,* or "change," is composed of the sun and moon. The relation of sun and moon symbolizes neverending change. According to the *I ching* the sun changes night to day and the moon changes day to night. By the interchanging of days and nights, the four seasons are formed, and by the changing of the seasons all things change. When the sun reaches its zenith, it begins to decline. When the moon is full, it wanes again. When night deepens, the day dawns. Living things are born and grow, decay and die. From solar systems to electrons, everything is in motion, everything changes. The world is transitory. As Confucius said, "Like the river, everything is flowing on ceaselessly, day and night."[7] The universe is in constant flux, a continuously procreative organism. As the great commentary to the *I ching* says, "The process of production and reproduction is what is called change."[8] The world is constantly in process of evolvement because of change occurring in all things. Since change (*i*) is responsible for the changing world, it is the ultimate reality, which is also known as *t'ai chi* (the "Great Ultimate").

THE *YIN* AND *YANG* PRINCIPLES

As indicated above, the word *change,* or *i* (易), consists of the sun (日) and the moon (月), and 月 is believed to be a variant form of the archaic pictogram 勿 . According to the *Ta chuan,* "The *yin* [dark principle] and *yang* [light principle] are correlated with the moon and the sun."[9] Therefore the sun came to be called *t'ai yang* ("great light") and the moon *t'ai yin* ("great darkness"). The sun and moon became prototypes of *yang* and *yin.* This idea is present in the *ho t'u,* or "river map," from which the *I ching* was believed to be derived.[10]

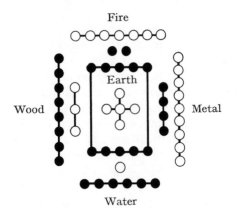

The map consists of light (*yang*) and dark (*yin*) circles. The light circles represent the sunlike character of *yang*, and the dark circles the moonlike character of *yin*. Combinations of circles, however, could not efficiently represent all the phenomena of changing process.[11] Therefore, lines were substituted for circles: unbroken lines for the light circles and broken lines for the dark circles. The solid line (——) signified *yang* and the broken line (— —) *yin* in the *I ching*.

These two primordial forces are the components of change. When the creative *(yang)* and the receptive *(yin)* interact, change occurs. If there were no *yin* and *yang*, there could be no change.[12] Thus "the Master [Confucius] said, the creative [*yang*] and the receptive [*yin*] are the gateway to change."[13] *Yin* and *yang* are the two cardinal principles of all existence. Nothing exists without them. *Yin's* attributes are femaleness, responsiveness, cold, north, earth, etc., and *yang's* are maleness, creativity, warmth, south, heaven, etc. Everything can be reduced to *yin* and *yang*. These forces, however, are not a duality, because they do not conflict with but complement each other. Neither can exist without the other. As we see from the symbols of *yin* (— —) and *yang* (——), they are different manifestations of one essence. *Yin* is *yang* divided, and *yang* is *yin* united. The condition of separation makes *yin* possible, just as the condition of unity makes *yang* possible.

In other words the distinctions between them are conditional and existential, not essential. *Yin* and *yang* are one in essence but two in existence. *Yin* always changes to *yang* by union, and *yang* changes to *yin* by separation. Union occurs through the expansion of *yin* and separation through the contraction of *yang*. Thus there is pattern in the process of change. The Great Commentary remarks, "When the sun goes, the moon comes. When the moon goes, the sun comes. The alternation of sun and moon produces light. When cold goes, heat comes. When heat goes, cold comes. The alternation of cold and heat completes the year. What is going contracts. What is to come expands. The alternation of contraction and expansion produces progression."[14]

It is, then, the alternation of expansion and contraction, or growth and decay, that makes possible the union of the separated and the separation of the united. When things have expanded to their maximums, they must contract. When they have contracted to their minimums, they must expand again. The alternating expansion and contraction is the pattern of changing process that is expressed in the alternation of *yin* and *yang* and symbolized by the union and separation of lines in the *I ching*. The broken line that is *yin* is known in Chinese as *jou hsiao* (柔 爻), the "soft" or "tender" line, while the unbroken *yang* line is *kang hsiao* (剛 爻), the "hard" or "firm" line. It is the natural tendency of the soft, or *yin*, line to grow together to form the unbroken *yang* line. It is equally natural for the *yang* line, which is hard, to break easily and thereby divide again. Thus alternating growth and decay, or expansion and contraction, are expressed by the union and separation of line, that is, by the alteration of *yin* to *yang* and of *yang* to *yin*. Through this alteration everything changes. Thus the interplay of *yin* and *yang* is the mechanism of change.

DUOGRAMS AND TRIGRAMS

The basic patterns of growth and decay or expansion and contraction are clearly depicted in the duograms, which are all the possible two-line combinations of *yin* and/or *yang*. Let us begin with new, as yet incomplete *yin* (⚏). When it has matured to its maximum, it becomes old *yin* (⚏), ready to begin yielding to the new *yang* (⚎), which is at its minimum. The new *yang* in turn matures to its maximum, becoming old, complete *yang* (⚌). The old *yang* then changes to the new *yin* (⚏), the minimum degree of *yin*, which in turn becomes the old *yin*, and the cycle of expansion and contraction recurs. Thus it is said, "The change is in the Great Ultimate, which generates the two primary forms [*yin* and *yang*]. The two primary forms produce the four images [the four duograms]. The four images produce the eight trigrams."[15]

The trigrams, which are all the possible three-line combinations of *yin* and/or *yang*, are the basic symbols of all possible situations in the universe. The expansion and contraction of one *yin* and one *yang* line creates the four duograms. The expansion and contraction of three-line combinations of *yin* and/or *yang* creates eight trigrams. These eight trigrams are prototypes of hexagrams in the *I ching*. Hexagrams are "double trigrams," known in Chinese as *chung kua* (重卦).[16] The sixty-four hexagrams in the *I ching*, which represent the germinal situations of all changing phenomena, constitute all the possible combinations of the eight trigrams.

While *yin* and *yang* represent the ontological foundation of all existence, the eight trigrams represent the functional foundations of all processes. The trigram is created by adding either a *yin* or a *yang* line to a duogram. It contains no "new" line or element. Its basic constituents remain *yin* and *yang*, which are the bases of all things. The trigrams express *yin-yang* interactions and their results. *Yin-yang* interplay inevitably creates either *yin* or *yang* in the continuing process of change. Because each interaction of *yin* and *yang* by nature produces another state, the trigram is functionally necessary to represent the process of change. The origin seems to be also related to the Chinese trinity, which is heaven, earth, and man, and it symbolizes completion. In it, man, the central line of the trigram, is the product of heaven (*yang*) and earth (*yin*). Here man is not ontologically different from heaven and earth; man's position constitutes his uniqueness. In this respect, the permutations of the duogram represent states of existence; the addition of another *yin* or *yang* line to these permutations of the duogram represents functional change.

The eight trigrams that represent the basic units of all cosmic phenomena are obtained by adding to each duogram another *yin* or *yang* line. If we add a *yang* line above a new *yin* (⚏), we obtain the trigram *sun* (☴), meaning "gentleness" and also called the "first daughter." If we add a *yin* line above a new *yin*, we obtain the trigram *k'an* (☵), meaning "abyss" or the "second son." If we add a *yang* line above an old *yin* (⚌), we get the trigram *ken* or "stillness" (☶), also called the "last son." By adding a *yin* line instead, we get the trigram *k'un* (☷), which is "earth" or the "mother." By the same process we can obtain the rest of the eight trigrams: *ch'ien* (☰), "heaven," or the "father"; *tui* (☱), "joyous," or "last daughter"; *li* (☲), fire or "second daughter"; and *chen* (☳), "awakening," or the "first son" in the family structure. These eight trigrams symbolize various attributes that can be combined to represent all possible situations in the universe. They correlate with directions, seasonal changes, personal characteristics, socio-political situations, and all other phenomena of the cosmos.[17]

HEXAGRAMS

Hexagrams are simply two trigrams combined. All possible combinations of the eight trigrams make sixty-four hexagrams. Hexagrams are sometimes called "great trigrams," or *ta sheng kua* (大 成 卦), and trigrams can be called "small hexagrams," or *hsiao sheng kua* (小 成 卦). The difference between them is not qualitative, merely quantitative, and, like *yin* and *yang*, each is essential to the existence of the other. Just as neither *yin* nor *yang* can exist without the other, one trigram alone does not represent a whole germinal situation in the universe. Just as *yin* and *yang* are complementary, so also are two trigrams in a hexagram.

The relationship of hexagrams to trigrams is well illustrated in the Great Commentary: "The *I ching* is a book that is vast and great and contains everything. It has the *tao* of heaven, the *tao* of the earth, and the *tao* of man. These three primal powers are doubled and make six lines. The six lines are nothing other than the *tao* of the three primal powers."[18] The hexagram is not merely the combination of two trigrams; it is also a separate entity. It can be compared with an atom, which comprises electrons and nucleus but is unique in itself. As atoms are the microcosms and building-blocks of the universe, hexagrams represent all the germinal situations in the universe. The sixty-four hexagrams contain everything. Thus it is said, "The *I ching* contains the measure of heaven and earth. Thus it enables us to conceive the *tao* of heaven and earth."[19]

Since the *I ching*, the sixty-four hexagrams, represents the universe in microcosm, to know the *I ching* is to know the universe. These hexagrams represent the changing germinal patterns of the universe. To know them is to know the processes of change. Each primal pattern of change, that is, each hexagram, is unique, but its uniqueness must be understood in its relationship to the whole. In other words, each hexagram is understood in its relation to other hexagrams. Everything in the whole process of change is interdependent and complementary. This kind of metaphysical and cosmological system is certainly compatible with the contemporary view of the world. This brief summary of the *I ching's* metaphysics of existence and change may be helpful in discussing the implications of the *I ching* for the Christian concept of God.

In examining various attributes of God in terms of the metaphysics of the *I ching*, I have employed the standard traditional and contemporary tenets of Christian thought. It is not my intention to ignore existing Christian traditions but to bring eastern philosophy to bear upon them. We must use past insights creatively to formulate new insights and reshape our beliefs according to the demands of our time. In so doing we become aware of similarities among different traditions.

This book is based upon the metaphysics of the *I ching*. Other eastern philosophic tenets are used to support or illustrate my basic hypothesis. Each essay in this book has been written as an integral unit, necessitating a certain amount of repetition of the metaphysical principle of the *I ching*. Such repetition will be helpful to western readers unfamiliar with the *I ching* and will be particularly convenient for readers interested in only certain of the essays. These essays are directed to theologians and theological students, Christian ministers, students of comparative religion, and informed lay people interested in a Christian concept of God from an eastern perspective.

Notes

1. See J. Y. Lee, "The Yin-Yang Way of Thinking," *International Review of Mission* 60 (July 1971):364.

2. The *I ching* originated in early divination in China. The formation of hexagrams and arrangements in the present text is traditionally attributed to King Wen, the founder of the Chou dynasty, and the appendix of ten wings is attributed to Confucius, even though King Wen and Confucius had very little to do with the formation of the book. However, the *I ching* was canonized and became one of the Confucian classics. See J. Y. Lee, "Some Reflections on the Authorship of the *I ching*," *Numen: International Review for the History of Religions* 17, fasc. 3 (December 1970):200–10.

3. See J. Y. Lee, *The Principle of Changes: Understanding the I Ching* (New Hyde Park, New York: University Books, 1971), pp. 40ff.

4. In his address "In Memory of Richard Wilhelm," delivered in Munich, May 10, 1930. It is reprinted in the Appendix of *The Secret of the Golden Flower*, trans. Richard Wilhelm (New York: Harcourt, Brace and World, 1962).

5. Ibid.

6. Lee, *The Principle of Changes*, p. 57.

7. *Analects*, 9:16.

8. *Ta chuan*, sec. 1, ch. 5.

9. Ibid., sec. 1, ch. 6.

10. This map was believed to be the work of Fu Hsi, the legendary culture hero, to whom the authorship of the *I ching* was often attributed. Many scholars, however, believe that the map was a creation of the Later Han period, when the *yin-yang* schools of philosophy were prevalent. See Lee, "Some Reflections on the Authorship of the *I Ching*," pp. 200–10, or *The Principle of Changes*, pp. 14–27.

11. See Lee, *The Principle of Changes*, p. 98.

12. *Ta chuan*, sec. I, ch. 12.

13. Ibid., sec. II, ch. 16.

14. Ibid., sec. II, ch. 5.

15. Ibid., sec. I, ch. 11.

16. See Lee, *The Principle of Changes,* pp. 106ff.

17. For additional attributes of trigrams see *Shuo kua* ("Discussion of the Trigrams"), which is the eighth "wing" of the *I ching.*

18. *Ta chuan,* sec. II, ch. 10.

19. Ibid., sec. I, ch. 4.

CHAPTER I

THEOLOGY OF CHANGE:
THE QUEST OF ITS METHODOLOGY

ORIENTATIONS OF TRADITIONAL THEOLOGY

Christian theology has been deeply influenced by Greek philosophy. Christianity was born in the Greek world and formulated by the Greek mind. The Greek way of thinking became the foundation of Christian theology in the West. For example, the trinitarian dogma formulated in the fourth and fifth centuries was based on the concept of substance, which is the basis of Greek ontology. Adolph Harnack, one of the great church historians of the West, pointed out the dominant influence of Greek philosophy on Christianity, distinguishing between the essence of Christianity and the doctrinal beliefs of the church.[1] The simple message of Christianity was transmuted into the metaphysical dogmas of the church through the intellectual apparatus of Greek philosophy.

Greek philosophy has played an important role throughout the history of Christian thought. St. Augustine, for example, constructed his theological system on the framework of Neoplatonism, as Thomas Aquinas constructed Roman Catholic theology on a framework of Aristotelianism. Thus Hellenistic philosophy, as Harnack says, "takes the form, not of a Christian product in Greek dress, but of a Greek product in Christian dress."[2] Reformers like Luther and Calvin re-examined the Scriptures and the works of Augustine but did not attempt to eliminate the influence of Greek philosophy from the Christian concept of God. The Cartesian reform was important in the development of

11

modern philosophy and mathematical science, but its rigorous dualism, based on a static worldview, was a refinement of Platonic philosophy. Even though contemporary ideas of God have been cast in many different philosophic molds (the Hegelian essence of the dialectic process, the Kierkegaardian realism of subjectivity, the Kantian synthetic forms of categorical understanding, or the Heideggerian autonomy of authentic existence), they all conceive of God as the essence of being, the fundamental category of Platonic and Aristotelian thinking. In that sense it is true, as Whitehead says, that all western philosophies are footnotes to Plato. Despite contemporary emphasis on the dynamic aspects of ontology, most of us remain imprisoned by the static concept of being.

Recently the so-called neo-orthodox or neo-Reformation theology has been prominent in the West. One of its outstanding proponents was Karl Barth, who was motivated by reaction against the liberal theology of the nineteenth century and the rise of the Nazi regime in Germany. Barth and his followers stressed the pure word of God, distinguishing it from Greek metaphysics. In order to strip Christianity of Greek metaphysics, Barth came close to declaring theology irreconcilable with philosophy. In the first volume of *Church Dogmatics* he speaks of the analogy of being, because of its derivation from Greek metaphysics, as an anti-Christ, an enemy of Christ. Barth attempted to replace the analogy of being with the analogy of relation but was not totally successful.[3] Despite Barth's endeavor to strip his theology of its Greek metaphysical aspects, he was accused by a conservative theologian, Cornelius van Til, of using Kantian categories of thinking in his theology.

Neo-orthodox theology is antimetaphysical, but new syntheses of philosophy and theology have also been attempted. For example, Bultmann attempted to integrate Heidegger's existential philosophy into his interpretation of the Christian message.[4] Tillich, on the other hand, has used dynamic ontology to construct a different synthesis of philosophy and theology. There have been other recent theological developments as well. The death-of-God theology has been prominent in America, as well as the theology of hope. All these types of theology, reflecting the temper of time, stress the dynamic aspect of God, but none of them breaks radically with the static ontology of Greek philosophy.

PROCESS THEOLOGY AND THEOLOGY OF CHANGE

It is important, however, to observe the growing trend of process theology in this country. This theology is quite different from traditional theistic theologies. It is, in fact, a radical departure from the static ontology that has dominated western thought for many centuries. Contemporary science made the growing interest in process theology almost inevitable. Static ontology, which is based on a static worldview, is untenable in the light of quantum theory and the theory of relativity. Process theology attempts to present the Christian faith in light of a relativistic and organic worldview, which is not only attuned to the contemporary scientific worldview but also to the traditional eastern worldview. Process theology, as Norman Pittenger says, arose from Whitehead's idea that the world is "alive."[5] Process theology may have a dominant influence on the future development of theology in America. It seems to provide more constructive and relevant alternatives than neo-orthodox and existentialist approaches to theology. Innovative theology, which has usually originated in Europe and been transmitted to North America, may be about to reverse direction.[6]

Process theology, while sharing in many respects the eastern worldview, is not identical with the eastern approach to theology. The organic worldview held for centuries in the East, mainly in India and China, presupposes a cyclic view of time, while the organic worldview of process philosophy presupposes a linear concept of time. The cyclic time of eastern cosmology is sharply differentiated from the linear concept of time that moves toward the novelty of creative process. The Hindu and Buddhist *kalpa* ("eon") is cyclic—like the year, although infinitely longer. In the cosmology of the *I ching* the archetypes, or germinal situations, represented by the sixty-four different hexagrams (each consisting of six broken and/or unbroken lines) remain the same, even though they manifest themselves differently in the world. Therefore the movement of time can be best expressed by the cyclic formation of hexagrams devised by Shao Yung (1011–77):

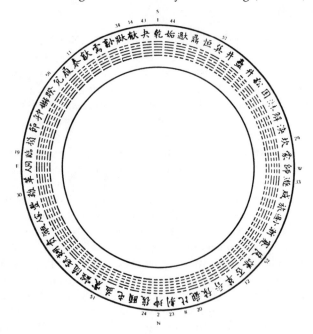

As we observe from the diagram of Shao Yung, time moves as *yang* (the undivided line) changes to *yin* (the divided line) and back again. In this process of change time moves in a complete circle and then repeats the same course. The cyclic movement of time is characteristic of eastern cosmology. Process philosophy, on the other hand, which currently dominates western cosmology, presupposes an ever-evolving process toward a higher realm of existence. Basic to Whitehead's vision is the creative advance into novelty. Meaning is found in a forward rather than a cyclic movement of time. This difference in their concepts of time clearly differentiates the theology of process from the theology of change: The former presupposes a linear concept of time, the latter a cyclic concept.

There are more differences, however, between the theology of change and the theology of process than their concepts of time.

There is also a difference in their use of the category "process." Process presupposes creativity, which is regarded as an ultimate reality by process theology.[7] But creativity, according to the *I ching*, presupposes change, the ultimate reality, which also includes receptivity (receptive capacity). In this respect, the ultimate reality includes not only the creative process but the receptive process as well. Thus the term "process" is less expressive than the idea of *i*, or change, as the ultimate category of reality.

In this respect, Paul Tillich agrees: "The term 'process' is much less equivocal than the term 'life' but also much less expressive."[8] Tillich, in the last volume of *Systematic Theology*, uses the term "life" for ultimate reality, but he fails to convince. The word "life" seems more constricted than the word "process." Life is the process of actualization. Actualization presupposes change. If the world is in process of realization toward its newness or its potentiality, this certainly presupposes the deeper reality that makes the creative process possible.

This deeper reality that generates the creative process is described in the *I ching* as change itself. According to the *I ching*, the process of creativity presupposes the reality of change that is changeless.[9] As Chang Chung-yuan said, "To understand the complete process of creation we have to understand, as well, the concept of the changeless within the ever-changing."[10]

In other words, the category of change in the *I ching* is a priori to what Whitehead calls the "creative advance into novelty."[11] As the Great Commentary to the *I ching* says, "The Great Ultimate is in the *i* [change]. It produces the two primary forms. The two primary forms produce the four images. The four images produce the eight trigrams" (*Ta chuan*, sec. I, ch. 11). The eight trigrams produce the sixty-four hexagrams, which represent all things in the universe.[12] The two primary forms (or categories) are creativity (the great *yang*, symbolized in the first hexagram, *ch'ien*, or heaven) and receptivity (the great *yin*, symbolized in the second hexagram, *k'un*, or earth). In other words, it is not the creative process that produces changes but change that produces creativity, the great *yang*, in process of becoming. According to the *I ching*, then, it is change, not process, that is the ultimate, noncontingent reality.

One of the more significant differences between the theology of change and other forms of theology is its logic. From its past the western world has inherited a predilection for exclusive and absolute categories, and these still dominate western theology. Western science, which was characteristically exclusive and absolute, derived from Aristotelian logic and Euclidean geometry, and even Newtonian physics did not create a radical change in western patterns of thought. Newton, for example, conceived of time and space as absolute, a priori, and exclusive categories. But Einstein's theory of relativity and Planck's quantum theory have radically altered the scientific, if not the popular, worldview. According to the theory of relativity the universe is constantly in the process of becoming. Time and space are not independent of each other but dependent and inclusive. Everything is in the process of becoming; nothing is stationary. Aristotelian logic, which bases its categorical exclusivism on the static worldview of the Eleatic and Platonic schools, is called in question by this new worldview:

Planck's quantum theory and Einstein's theory of relativity led to the Aristotelian "either-or" being questioned. The result of the first was that the axiom, *natura non facit saltus* (nature makes no leaps), became untenable. As a consequence of the quantum theory, we know today that nature is very capable of making such leaps. This was the first intrusion into the Aristotelian "either-or." . . . We know today that matter is not merely a spatial element but also a temporal one. It is corpuscular as well as wave-like, so that both are merely different aspects of the same thing. In "this as well as that" lies the decisive impetus which has led to questioning the Aristotelian "either-or."[13]

Aristotelian "either-or" logic presupposes an absolutely dualistic worldview, which is contradicted by the idea of mutual interdependency. Even though modern science has revolutionized its worldview, this seems not to have altered conventional thinking. Most western theologians are still proponents of Aristotelian logic. As Wilfred Smith has pointed out, we in the West "presume that an intelligent man must choose: *either* this *or* that."[14] Perhaps, as Dr. Chang says,"Intellection is necessarily dualistic because it always implies subject and object.[15]

"Either-or" logic has been so deeply rooted in the intellectual life of the West that it seems almost impossible to overcome in theology.

This centuries-old western propensity to think in terms of "either-or" is not easily eliminated from process philosophy. Whitehead, who is aware of this problem, notes that the Aristotelian emphasis on the "subject-predicate" form of proposition is primarily responsible for the error of the Aristotelian notion of "substance."[16] But although Whitehead perceives the danger of separating subject and object, he does not always avoid it. Instead of observing "reality as it is in its totality and wholeness," "Whitehead . . . takes the universal dependent co-origination or creative flux as the occasion for probing into reality by the analytic and automical methods that have been so successful in the sciences."[17] Since the analytic method presupposes the exclusive way of thinking, Whitehead is not totally free from "either-or" thinking. But if ultimate reality transcends the distinction between subject and object, it is not possible to describe it by the logic of "either-or." To eliminate the Aristotelian "either-or" from theology is to accept the idea that ultimate truth lies not in "either-or" but in "this as well as that." Or, as Wilfred Smith said, "In all ultimate matters, truth lies not in an either-or, but in a both-and."[18]

Whitehead seems to be aware of the dipolarity of divine nature, which is expressed in terms of *both* the primordial *and* consequent nature.[19] But, as John Cobb points out, Whitehead then seems to separate God's primordial nature from his consequent nature; Whitehead fails to describe God in the most inclusive terms, the continuum of "both-and" and "this as well as that." Whitehead also separates the world from God: "God and the World are the contrasted opposites in terms of which creativity achieves its supreme task of transforming disjoined multiplicity, with its diversities in opposition, into concrescent unity, with its diversities in contrast."[20] If God is the contrasted opposite of the world, he can be both the world and God at the same time, but to conceive God as the contrasted opposite of the world in fact presupposes dualistic logic. God, if he is ultimate, must be seen as the totality of all creative process, rather than as a contrasted opposite of it. If God is the ultimate reality, he must be ultimate *both* in actuality *and* in potentiality. Limiting God's actuality of necessity creates a dualistic outlook. The God who transcends the Aristotelian "either-or" is not only the "becoming" God but also the "being" God. He is *both* process *and* state, *both* organic *and* inorganic, *both* creative *and* destructive, and *both* generation *and* degeneration. This principle—the inclusive "this as well as that" or "both-and"—underlies the theology of change and differentiates it from process theology.

The *I ching*'s concept of change as the ultimate reality must be understood in light of this inclusive way of thinking. In other words, change as the ultimate reality is always conceived in terms of simultaneous change *and* changelessness. Likewise the process of becoming presupposes the state of being. The one does not replace the other; they coexist. Just as change presupposes changelessness, becoming presupposes being. Paul Tillich's criticism of process theology has some validity when he says, "I must confess that I find this ontological analysis very attractive (being and action are two aspects of the prius of thinking), more so than the related attempts of Whitehead and Hartshorne to replace 'being' by 'becoming' as the character of the ultimate."[21]

In the philosophy of the *I ching* "being" cannot be replaced by "becoming," because they coexist. Change, which is an inclusive, or "both-and," category is, according to the Great Commentary on the *I ching*, a more ultimate reality than creativity: "Change generates the two primary forces,"[22] the forces of heaven and earth. Heaven here seems to correspond to Whitehead's idea of God, and earth to his idea of the World. Creativity comes from the interaction between heaven and earth or between God and World. Thus, according to the *I ching*, it is change that produces both concrescent poles of creativity. Change as the ultimate is more than a part of the creative process. It is the very source and ground of every creative act of actual becoming in the present and the future. Change that is both being and becoming can transcend not only the idea of a limited God but the idea of dualism between the World and God. Thus the theological ultimate reality of the *I ching* is not creativity but change that is also changless. Process theology in this respect presupposes theology of change, for change is the a priori category of process and creativity.

Theology of change is then quite different from and more fundamental than process theology, because it deals with the root of process, that is, change. The three characteristic forms of theological thinking we can label, for convenience' sake, the theology of the absolute, the theology of process, and the theology of change. Process theology can be understood as a transitional theology, standing between the traditional Christian theology of substance and the eastern theology of change. In the theology of the absolute the concept of unchanging being characterizes the ultimate, or God. The theology of the absolute derives from Greek philosophy, particularly Eleatic and Platonic metaphysics. As Thorleif Boman points out,[23] Plato, for example, conceived of reality in terms of unchanging being. The good is defined as the perfection of being, God himself. The Aristotelian definition of God as the "unmoved mover" is clearly a forerunner of the theology of substance. As Whitehead points out, the theology of the absolute or of a static being, in which fact is ultimate, has been dominant in the West, while the theology of process, in which becoming is ultimate, is more closely associated with the East.[24] Tillich's definition of God as being itself seems to characterize the ultimate category of reality as being rather than becoming. Tillich's ontology, however, is not static but dynamic.[25]

In the theology of process becoming is the character of the ultimate. God is known in the process of becoming rather than in the state of being. Becoming is the basic category of Hebrew thought, as being is basic to Greek.[26] The idea of becoming, however, presupposes being. Tillich declares that: "Hartshorne, in many discussions, has never convinced me that his doctrine of a 'becoming God' could express the religious experience of the eternity and majesty of the divine."[27] I in turn find Tillich's characterization of the divine in terms of being as incomplete as Tillich finds Hartshorne's use of becoming as the ultimate category. Process theology, or theology of becoming, is incomplete.

We need a theology that encompasses *both* "being" *and* "becoming" as the ultimate character of reality. Reality in an ultimate sense is not known in an "either-or" but in a *"both-and."*

"Both-and" philosophy is based on the idea of change, which produces both *yin* and *yang*. *Yin* is rest, *yang* is movement; *yin* is being, *yang* is becoming. *Yin* is responsiveness, *yang* is creativity. If creativity is the character of the ultimate in process theology, responsiveness is the character of the ultimate in substantial or absolute theology. If *yang* is the leitmotiv of process theology, *yin* is the leitmotiv of absolute theology. Theology of change, however, comprises both *yin* and *yang*, both creativity and responsiveness, both being and becoming, because change is the source of both. Change is, then, the matrix of all that was, is, and shall be. It is the ground of all being and becoming. Thus theology of change, which characterizes the ultimate as being *and* becoming, is that inclusive theology to which we must turn. Process theology represents the turning away from western absolute theology toward the eastern theology of change.

THE THEOLOGY OF CHANGE AS VALID THEOLOGY

James Joyce once said that the West shall shake the East awake, but the West will have the night for morn. If we believe that the theology of substance of unchanging being has been closely associated with the western mind, and theology of change with eastern thought, it was a profound prediction. The theology of unchanging being is on the verge of transition to the theology of change by way of the theology of process. Theology of being and theology of becoming, both western in origin, can both be comprised and come to fulfillment in the eastern theology of change. Should this occur, the western bud of Christian theology will have flowered by means of eastern philosophy. Theology of change can be theology of the future and fulfillment. Theology of the future is not a theology of hope but a theology of ultimate evolvement. In the theology of change, change is the ultimate category of all things, organic or inorganic, spiritual or material, form or matter, being or becoming, for *yin* and *yang* are the dipolar categories of all things. The theology of change is the theology of fulfillment. This theology is then ecumenical theology, or theology for all religions; relevant theology, or theology expressive of the contemporary worldview; and ecological theology, or theology of both human beings and nature. Let me elaborate on the theology of change as an ecumenical theology, a relevant theology, and an ecological theology.

Ecumenical theology must be based on a metaphysical symbol rather than on cultural or devotional symbols that are meaningful only in their own milieus. Change is a metaphysical symbol applicable to any situation or discipline. Because of its universality, it is inherently ecumenical. The concept of change is the most inclusive and ecumenical category of thought—the "both-and," or "*yin-yang*" category.[28] The inclusiveness inherent in the concept of change renders the theology of change inclusive and ecumenical. Theology based on exclusive patterns of thought cannot by definition be ecumenical, because exclusive logic is based on the famous tenet "*tertium non datur*" (there is no third). "In other words, either something is or it is not; there is no other possibility."[29] The most inclusive way of thinking, that is, the "*yin-yang*" way of thinking, allows a third possibility.

Christianity's original message was inclusive; it developed into an exclusive religion because of the exclusiveness—the *tertium non datur*—of western philosophy, which became its medium. Christianity's exclusiveness has always been clearly evident in its relations with other religions. Because of the exclusivist philosophy through which its theology was expressed, Christianity was bound to stress conversion of non-Christians rather than cultivation of goodness in whatever guise, and to stress expansion at the expense of other religions rather than cooperation and dialogue with them. Theology of change, however, which makes use of the most inclusive category of "both-and," can encompass all existing religions, because it encompasses the complementarity of all opposites and concrescent poles for the creative integration of the whole.

The uniqueness of Christianity lies in its inclusiveness rather than in its exclusive claim to authority. Certainly the theology of change universalizes Christianity by acknowledging the universality of other religions. It encourages not competition but cooperation, not domination but coordination, not authority but authenticity, not conformity but affirmation. It rejects strict dualism—a dualism that is in any case incompatible with the original Judeo-Christian message—even though it allows dualism in a relative sense. Change is simultaneously transcendent and immanent. Its transcendence makes immanence possible, and its immanence makes transcendence possible. Moreover it comprises personal and impersonal reality. Since ultimate reality is beyond intellectual formulation, in the Upanishads it is often called "*neti, neti*" ("neither this nor that"), a phrase intended to convey that what is being described is in fact beyond description. "Neither-nor" should be understood as a negative counterpart of "both-and."[30] Because ultimate reality transcends description, it is often referred to in both its personal and impersonal aspect simply as "it."

Change in the *I ching* is certainly beyond categorization. It is simultaneously personal and impersonal, male and female, immanent and transcendent. It has been classically defined as "change: that is the unchangeable."[31] The *I ching* says, "Change means no thought and no anxiety. When it is silent, it is immovable; when it moves, it penetrates to all things in the universe."[32] Change is both changing and unchanging, because it is both *yin*, rest, and *yang*, movement. Just as change includes being and becoming, the theology of change includes the traditional theology of being and the contemporary theology of becoming. It also includes all forms of religious expression, for it is itself the most inclusive category. That is why theology of change is ecumenical; it transcends particular religious beliefs and practices.

The theology of change is also relevant to the contemporary worldview, which is quite different from the classical western worldview based on Euclidean geometry. The classical western worldview, which many of us still take for granted, is mechanistic, materialistic, and deterministic. In this worldview time and space are regarded as independent and everything is ruled by the inexorable law of cause and effect. It is unfortunate that so many contemporary theologians still think in these terms. The world perceived by contemporary science is not the static, Euclidean world but the moving and dynamic world of relativity. Einstein's theory of relativity and the new nuclear physics ushered in a radically new worldview in which everything, including time and space, is interdependent and complementary. That is why

Wilfred C. Smith believes that the twentieth-century view of the world is approaching the idea of change expressed in the *I ching*.[33] The world we live in is in constant change because of change. Change is the basis of a changing world. The components of this kind of world are organisms that are also in constant transformation. "Biology is the study of the larger machine, whereas physics is the study of the smaller organisms."[34] The organic form of world that is constantly changing must be the basis for our understanding of inorganic forms of existence. In this worldview everything is mutually independent and complementary. The changing organic world is described in terms of growth and decay. The fundamental assumption of our contemporary, relativistic worldview is that the world is constantly in process of becoming. The theology that accepts this assumption and this worldview is the theology of change.

It might be asked whether one's worldview does in fact determine one's method of theological inquiry. The task of theology is primarily to interpret ultimate reality to the people of its time. Since any interpretation must perforce be expressed by imageries taken from the world, the kind of worldview we hold certainly affects our understanding of ultimate reality. Even though some theologians stubbornly insist that our perception of the divine comes directly from God, there is no way for us to express this perception except by imageries and symbols borrowed from our perception of the world. Karl Barth attempted to make theology independent of human expression, but he failed. He finally admitted that the word of man is necessary to receive the Word of God.[35] We know that it is almost impossible to understand New Testament theology without knowing the worldview of those times, because the theology was conditioned by and expressed in the terms of the worldview.

One of Rudolf Bultmann's most profoundly innovative suggestions is that the New Testament must be "demythologized" before it can serve us as a work of theology.[36] "Demythologizing" meant, essentially, reinterpreting the New Testament message in terms of the scientific worldview of our time.[37] "The cosmology of the New Testament," Bultmann says, "is essentially mythical in character. The world is viewed as a three-storied structure, with the earth in the center, the heaven above, and the underworld beneath. Heaven is the above of God and of celestial beings—the angels. The underworld is hell, the place of torment. Even the earth is more than the scene of natural, everyday events, of the trivial round and common task."[38] Bultmann realized that since the worldview expressed in the New Testament had been radically changed by science, the concept of God and salvation expressed in terms of the New Testament worldview was almost completely untenable in the modern world.

The worldview that Bultmann proposed, however, has also nearly become mythological and needs, in its turn, to be demythologized in light of the world of process and change. Process theology certainly takes account of the implications for theology of the relativistic world of our time. The radical change in worldview since Einstein and the development of nuclear physics has stimulated a radical change in theological method. Theology that is not in tune with its contemporary worldview is not relevant to the human experience of its time. Theology and worldview are mutually interdependent and must be mutually coherent. If process theology is based on the contemporary worldview, theology of change, which is the foundation of process, must be the theology of future and fulfillment.

The theology of fulfillment is also the theology of ecology, for the ecosystem includes everything that is. Whitehead's organic worldview has begun to be taken seriously in ecological study. The ecosystem can be compared with an organic system in which everything, organic or inorganic, is not only interdependent but forms a continuum. Humans are not separate from their environment; they are a part of nature and share existence in it with other parts. The ecological problem of our technological civilization can be primarily attributed to our exclusivistic approach to thinking based on our dualistic worldview.[39] To differentiate human existence from other existence is a form of dualism. To value the quality of human existence above the quality of other forms of existence creates inevitable conflict and disturbs the delicate ecosystem of the world. Traditional dualistic Christian theology was able to segregate men from—and exalt man over—nature by differentiating between personal and nonpersonal existence.

Perhaps this western dualism originated primarily in the belief in a personal God. The Judeo-Christian belief in a personal God as the ultimate reality is certainly the original cause of our ecological crisis. Tillich seems to have realized that when he redefined God so as to transcend the traditional concept of a personal God. God as ultimate reality transcends any categorization. God as "change itself" transcends the personal God as well as the impersonal God, because it includes both personal and impersonal God. Perhaps that is what Meister Eckhart meant when he said that the highest form of the divine is godhead, which is beyond the trinitarian gods. The God of Hebrews, who is beyond our understanding, is not categorized as either personal or impersonal, not limited by Aristotelian either-or logic. God is both-and, "I am who I am" (Exodus 3:14), or "I become who I become."[40]

God is something that logic fails to describe—the state or the process of undifferentiated continuum. This God is beyond attributes and beyond personal being. This attributeless God is change itself. Everything, whether personal or impersonal, changes because of change itself. Since everything changes, change itself is the most inclusive reality. Thus the theology of change is the theology of fulfillment for all, personal or impersonal. It deals with the wholeness of cosmos and the totality of ecosystem, in which human beings are a part. That is precisely why the theology of change is ecumenical theology, relevant theology, and ecological theology of the future.

Finally it may be asked why Christian theology should employ the eastern concept of change. Is it not a betrayal of the Christian faith to employ an idea out of another tradition? In response to this question we must remember that the *I ching* is not religious literature but wisdom literature. We are interested in its metaphysics, not its esoteric lore or its techniques of divination. The *I ching* is perhaps one of the earliest books to attempt an explanation of the cosmic patterns of change. It deals not with a sectarian god or form of worship but with the common and universal experience of cosmic change. Platonic and Aristotelian metaphysics, which have been the framework of traditional Christian theology, postulate being as the absolute category of reality; the *I ching* postulates change as the ultimate category of reality.

A variety of metaphysical systems have served as vehicles for the Christian faith. Christian theologians have used Platonic, or Aristotelian, or Kantian, or Cartesian, or Hegelian metaphysics to convey the idea of the ultimate reality, and in no case do we consider their metaphysics a betrayal of their Christian faith. If Christianity is truly not a sect but a universal religion, we have no reason to reject a clear and comprehensive interpretation of change simply because it originated in China. Chinese philosophy is as acceptable a vehicle for Christian faith as Greek philosophy. If it were not, Christianity would not be ecumenical and universal. To deny the ecumenicity and universality of Christianity is to deny the truth of Christianity, for truth lies not in the either-or but in the both-and category of thought.

In addition, scientific technology forces us to accept a universalistic worldview. In the space age the earth has become a global village. Revolutionary advances in transportation and communications are shrinking distances and differences between people. Christianity, like Hinduism and Buddhism, is a world religion. Thus there is no reason why Christian theology, which has been monopolized by Greek wisdom for so long, cannot now incorporate Chinese wisdom.

Perhaps it is time for the concept of change expressed in the *I ching* to integrate Christian theology and contemporary cosmology into a new expression of reality. Since the concept of change expressed in the *I ching* is not only compatible with the modern worldview but is the ultimate category of reality, the theology of change can be the most promising and acceptable form of Christian expression in the future.

Notes

1. See Adolph Harnack, *What is Christianity?* trans. Thomas B. Saunders (New York: Harper and Brothers, 1957).

2. Ibid., p. 221.

3. See J. Y. Lee, "Karl Barth's Use of Analogy in His Church Dogmatics," *Scottish Journal of Theology* 22, no. 2 (June 1969): 129–51.

4. See J. Y. Lee, "'Bultmann's Existentialist Interpretation and the Problem of Evil," *Journal of Religious Thought*, Autumn-Winter 1969, pp. 64–80.

5. Norman Pittenger, *God in Process* (London: SCM Press, 1967), p. 99.

6. Some prominent North American process theologians are Daniel Day Williams of Union Seminary in New York; John Cobb and David Griffin of Claremont, California; Schubert Ogden of Southern Methodist University; Bernard Meland of Chicago Divinity School; and Norman Pittenger, formerly of New York but now at Cambridge, England.

7. See Alfred North Whitehead, *Process and Reality: An Essay in Cosmology* (New York: Macmillan, 1957), pp. 10–11.

8. Paul Tillich, *Systematic Theology* (Chicago: University Press of Chicago, 1963), 3:11.

9. "Change that is also changeless" is a classical Chinese concept of change. It will be explained later in detail.

10. Chang Chung-yuan, *Creativity and Taoism: A Study of Chinese Philosophy, Art and Poetry* (New York: Julian Press, 1963), p. 72.

11. Ibid., p. 74.

12. J. Y. Lee, *The Principle of Changes: Understanding the I Ching* (New Hyde Park, New York: University Books, 1971), p. 89.

13. Jean Gebser in P. J. Saher, *Eastern Wisdom and Western Thought: A Comparative Study in the Modern Philosophy of Religion* (New York: Barnes and Noble, 1970), p. 10.

14. Wilfred Cantwell Smith, *The Faith of Other Men* (New York: New American Library, 1963), p. 72.

15. Chang Chung-yuan, *Creativity and Taoism*, p. 103.

16. Whitehead, *Process and Reality*, p. 45.

17. Ryusei Takeda and John B. Cobb, Jr., "*Mosa-Dharma* and Prehensions: A Comparison of Nāgārjuna and Whitehead," *Philosophy of Religion and Theology, 1973 Proceedings*, American Academy of Religion, p. 188.

18. Smith, *Faith of Other Men*, p. 72.

19. Whitehead, *Process and Reality*, p. 524.

20. Ibid., p. 528.

21. Paul Tillich, "Rejoinder," *Journal of Religion* 46 (January 1966): 185.

22. *Ta chuan*, sec. I, ch. 11.

23. Thorleif Boman, *Hebrew Thought Compared with Greek*, trans. Jules L. Moreau (London: SCM Press, 1960), pp. 53ff.

24. Whitehead, *Process and Reality*, p. 11.

25. Paul Tillich in the last volume of *Systematic Theology* stresses life rather than process as the ultimate category of theology. This shows his use of being as a dynamic expression of life.

26. Boman, *Hebrew Thought*, pp. 27ff.

27. Tillich, "Rejoinder," p. 187.

28. For a comprehensive discussion of the *"yin-yang"* way of thinking, see J. Y. Lee, *The I: A Christian Concept of Man* (New York: Philosophical Library, 1971), pp. 4–10; J. Y. Lee, "Yin-Yang Way of Thinking: A Possible Method for Ecumenical Theology," *International Review of Mission* 40, no. 239 (July 1971): 363–70.

29. Saher, *Eastern Wisdom and Western Thought*, p. 10.

30. Jean Gebser, "Foreword," Saher, ibid., p. 12.

31. J. Y. Lee, *The Principle of Changes*, pp. 70ff; J. Y. Lee, *The I: A Christian Concept of Man*, p. 6; Hellmut Wilhelm, *Change: Eight Lectures on the I Ching* (New York: The Bollingen Foundation, 1960), p. 23.

32. See Chang Chung-yuan, *Creativity and Taoism*, p. 86; Dr. Chang believes that the idea of changing-changelessness in the *I ching* derives from Taoism, but in fact the reverse is true. See J. Y. Lee, "Some Reflections on the Authorship of the *I ching*," *Numen*, December 1970, pp. 200–10.

33. Wilfred Smith, *Faith of Other Men*, p. 67.

34. Alfred N. Whitehead, *Science and the Modern World* (New York: Macmillan, 1925), p. 105.

35. J. Y. Lee, "Karl Barth's Use of Analogy in His Church Dogmatics," *Scottish Journal of Theology* 22, no. 2 (June 1969): 136–37.

36. The whole text of "New Testament and Mythology" is in Hans Werner Bartsch, ed., *Kerygma and Myth: A Theological Debate*, trans. by Reginald H. Fuller (London: SPCK, 1957), pp. 1–44.

37. J. Y. Lee, "Bultmann's Existentialist Interpretation," p. 67.

38. Bartsch, ed., *Kerygma and Myth*, p. 1.

39. Ecological crisis is commonly attributed to the outgrowth of western beliefs and attitudes regarding nature. See Lynn White, Jr., "The Historical Roots of our Ecological Crisis, *Science*, March 10, 1967, pp. 1203–7. Our beliefs and attitudes regarding nature are rooted, however, in our exclusive dualistic way of thinking.

40. The verb *hayah* here signifies becoming rather than being. See Boman, *Hebrew Thought*, pp. 38ff. It will be explained further in the next chapter.

CHAPTER II

CHANGE AS ULTIMATE REALITY: GOD AS CHANGE ITSELF

As we have indicated in the previous chapter, the traditional Christian concept of God has been much influenced by Greek metaphysics, particularly the philosophies of Plato and Aristotle. Neoplatonic philosophy provided a conceptual framework for Augustine's theology; the writings of Aquinas, which define and exemplify Catholic thinking, derive from Aristotelian metaphysics.

Early church fathers, such as Tertullian and Hippolytus, furiously attacked those who believed in the co-suffering of the Father with the Son. In this controversy Callistus, Praxeas, and Neotus were excommunicated as proponents of the patripassian heresy. According to the static ontology of Greek metaphysics the perfect God is not affected by passions or emotions. Thus "the doctrine of compassion or co-passion, namely Father suffering with the Son, has been declared heretical."[1] During the Middle Ages the doctrine of the impassibility of God, that is, that God is incapable of suffering, was defended by Thomas Aquinas. Aquinas based his opinion on the Aristotelian notion of God as the "immovable first mover," a term which implies divine perfection and immutability.[2] Since God is perfect, "only God is altogether unchangeable: creatures can all change in some way or other."[3] Things that change do so because of their potential for actualization.[4] By definition God does not have any passive potentiality: "God is sheer actuality, simply and wholly complete, and not wanting for anything."[5] Change is incompatible with divine nature, which is absolutely "unchangeable."[6] Even in this definition of God as the unchangeable being some notion of a dynamic nature is inherent, but the emphasis is on his immutability. The Aristotelian idea of God as the "unmoved mover," confirmed by Aquinas and reaffirmed by Descartes, is still accepted by most theologians.

This concept of God alters, however, if we change the frame of reference by which we understand the reality of God to a relativistic view of the world. Can God be understood as "change itself" rather than unchanging "being itself?" If the changing world of relativity instead of a static world of absolutes becomes the basis of one's thinking, it is possible to define God as the change that changes all changing phenomena. God can be conceived of as the "moving mover" or the "primordial change" if change is the underlying structure of reality. We shall see that "change itself" can be a more realistic definition of God than "being itself" or "becoming itself." This is not to deny that God is "being itself." Rather God is "being itself" because he is "change itself." He is the essence of being because he is primarily the essence of change.

THE NONSYMBOLIC NATURE OF GOD
IN JUDEO-CHRISTIAN TRADITION

Let us now examine whether the Judeo-Christian idea of God is compatible with the definition of God as "change itself." The God of Hebrews and Christians is known by many different names or symbols, among them "lord," "master," "father," "king," "creator," "love," "truth," "spirit," and "light." These names are symbolic reflections of certain conditions under which an encounter between divine and human nature took place. Our inquiry into the Judeo-Christian concept of God must begin with the idea of God that existed before the symbolization of God in human terms. That is, we must begin our investigation by examining the conception of God prior to God's symbolization.

The primordial idea of God is clearly expressed in Exodus 3:1–15, which describes the first confrontation between Moses and God. In this confrontation God announces his intention to bring his people out of slavery in Egypt under the leadership of Moses. God directs Moses to tell the people of Israel that he was sent by the God of their fathers. Moses answers, "If I come to the people of Israel and say to them, 'The God of your fathers has sent me to you,' and they ask me, "What is his name," what shall I say to them?" God replies, "I AM WHO I AM" (Exod. 3:13–14), and he adds, "Say this to the people of Israel, 'The Lord [YHWH], the God of your fathers, the God of Abraham, the God of Isaac, and the God of Jacob, has sent me to you' " (Exod. 3:15).

The significance of these passages is undeniable: They describe Moses' primordial experience with the God of Israel and give the origin of an early name for God. Later forms of God's name, such as king, lord, master, or savior, were determined by the demands with which people confronted God. Exodus 3:1–15 presents an unadorned description of the God of the Judeo-Christian tradition. Therefore it is of utmost importance for us clearly to comprehend this passage, for it reveals the real meaning of the divine being in the history of Judeo-Christian thought. In studying this passage, let us pay particular attention to its names for God: "I AM WHO I AM," which is used interchangeably with "YHWH." Alternative translations of this phrase are "I AM WHAT I AM," "I WILL BE WHAT I WILL BE,"[7] or "I BECOME WHAT I BECOME."[8] "YHWH" seems to derive from the Hebrew verb *hayah*, which can be translated as "to be," "to become," or "is-ness."[9] Therefore the meanings of "I AM WHAT I AM" and "YHWH" are identical, both terms designating the God of Abraham, Isaac, and Jacob.

The primordial idea of God is clearly expressed in Exodus 3:1–15. "I AM WHO I AM" or "I BECOME WHAT I BECOME" (*ehyeh aser ehyeh*) is the most profound, yet most ambiguous, term in the Old Testament. It is a mystical statement. At first impression it does not seem to explain anything about the nature of God and has often been interpreted as God's refusal to answer Moses' question: " 'I am who I am,' that is to say, 'I will not tell you my name.' "[10] But this is a questionable interpretation. Instead God's statement ought to be understood as signifying the impossibility of defining God in terms comprehensible to human beings. God is nameless and mysterious to humans, beyond human imagination and understanding and therefore beyond description and categorization.

Words cannot express his reality, and to attempt to describe him in human language is to make him less than God. For this reason many theologians, like Sören Kierkegaard, Rudolf Otto, and Karl Barth, have in the past tried to differentiate qualitatively between God's attributes and humankinds'. God is wholly other. As Jacob said, "God is found who in speaking of himself says: I am [*ehyeh*] and of whom men affirm: he is [*yihyeh*].[11] " God is nameless and without human attributes, yet the early church attempted to define what God ought to be by the words *tres personae* ("three persons") and *una substantia* ("one substance"). He is *mysterium logicum*, the mystery of God who is beyond human conceptualization. Because God eludes human imagery, there is no adequate symbol for him.

The name of God, that is, the symbol of God, is therefore ineffable. A definition of God as that which is, "is-ness itself," is a nonsymbolic statement, for it does not point beyond itself.[12] God as "is-ness itself" can transcend the dichotomy between essence and existence, subject and object. In this respect "I AM WHO I AM" affirms God's existence without making a statement about his nature. God is known only in terms of "I am" (*ehyeh*), or "he is" (*yihyeh*). That the emphasis is on "am-ness" or "is-ness" rather than "I" or "he" is made clear by the use of the term "YHWH," which is derived from the verb *hayah*, to be.[13] God as "is-ness itself" can be regarded as the primordial concept of God in the Judeo-Christian tradition, and one of the basic characteristics of this concept is, as we have indicated, its lack of symbolism.[14]

THE NONSYMBOLIC NATURE OF GOD
IN EASTERN TRADITIONS

The Upanishads also contain this kind of nonsymbolic statement to define the supreme reality. It cannot be known to us through our senses or our thoughts: "There the eye goes not; speech goes not, nor the mind. We know not, we understand not how one would teach it."[15] This supreme reality, or Brahman, cannot be postulated: "Not by speech, not by mind, not by sight can It be apprehended. How can It be comprehended otherwise than by one's saying 'It is!' "[16] There is no way to describe "it" other than in negative terms. Thus "it" is known through the famous double negation *neti, neti* ("neither this nor that"). The double negation is not a denial of its existence; it denies, rather, the ability of characteristics adequately to describe "it." This supreme reality is unthinkable, unimaginable, incomprehensible, and indescribable. It transcends the differentiation between existence and essence or between subject and object and is pure consciousness and the eternal subject. Brahman and YHWH are identical in being supreme reality that cannot be symbolized.

The nonsymbolic nature of nirvana is also affirmed in Buddhist teachings. Even though the idea of nirvana is hardly comparable to the Judeo-Christian idea of God,[17] it certainly represents the supreme reality in Buddhism. Etymologically *nirvana* means "to extinguish," particularly to extinguish the causes of suffering. Thus, a wanderer said to Reverend Sariputta: "Whatever, your reverence, is the extinction of passion, of aversion, of confusion, this is called Nirvana."[18] This state of extinction is "incomprehensible, indescribable, inconceivable, unutterable, for after we eliminate every aspect of the only consciousness we now know, how can we speak of what is left?"[19] In it "there is no coming or going or remaining or deceasing or uprising, for this is itself without support, without continuance, without mental object—this is itself the end of suffering."[20] Therefore Nagasena attempts to illustrate the nonsymbolic nature of nirvana by using wind as an analogy. He begins with the question: "Is there, sire, what is called wind?"

"Yes, revered sir."

"Please, sire, show the wind by its colour or configuration or as thin or long or short."

"But it is not possible, revered Nagasena, for the wind to be shown; for the wind cannot be grasped in the hand or touched; but yet there is wind."

"If, sire, it is not possible for the wind to be shown, well then, there is no wind."

"I, revered Nagasena, know that there is wind, I am convinced of it, but I am not able to show the wind."

"Even so, sire, there is Nirvana; but it is not possible to know Nirvana by colour or configuration."[21]

As Huston Smith said, "This indescribable character of Nirvana caused later Buddhists to speak of it as *Śūnyatā*, or 'emptiness.' It is not void or a negation of existence but it is empty in a way analogous to the way suprasonic is empty of sounds our ears can detect."[22] *Śūnyatā* is also called "suchness," "because one takes reality such as it is, without superimposing any ideas upon it."[23] Therefore the supreme reality in Buddhist tradition, whether called nirvana or *Śūnyatā*, is expressed in nonsymbolic terms. In this it is identical with Brahman and YHWH.

In the *Tao te ching* the nonsymbolic nature of the supreme reality is called *tao*, or "the way." Lao Tzu begins with the meaning of *tao*: "The *tao* that can be said is not the eternal *tao*, and the name that can be named is not the real name." *Tao* in this respect is indescribable and incomprehensible. It is beyond the understanding and classifications of human wisdom. That is why ninth-century T'ang poet Po Chu-i wrote of Lao Tzu and the *Tao te ching*:

Those who speak do not know;
Those who know do not speak.
This is what we were told by Lao Tzu.
Should we believe that he himself was the one who knew?
How could it then be that he wrote no less than five thousand words.[24]

Lao Tzu perhaps knew *tao's* is-ness, though its nature remains indescribable, even in "five thousand words." Imperfect containers of meaning words may be, nevertheless Taoists do use the word *tao* in the sense of "truth," "ultimate reality," "logos," etc.[25] The concept of *tao* in the *tao te ching* is more than the idea of God: it corresponds to Eckhart's concept of godhead.[26] What Lao Tzu attempts to say about *tao* implies the primordial expression of God, the is-ness of God that is beyond description. Thus Lao Tzu said, "When you look at it, you cannot see it; it is called formless. When you listen to it you cannot hear it; it is called soundless."[27] The *tao* is a void, used but never filled.[28] It is then identical with the idea of *śūnyatā,* or godhead, as "pure nothingness" (*ein bloss nicht*).[29] This inexpressible *tao* seems to imply the ultimate reality known as (Nirguna) Brahman, nirvana, *śūnyatā,* or YHWH. As Lao Tzu said, "Its true name we do not know; the *'Tao'* [Brahman, Nirvana, or YHWH] is the by-name we give it."[30]

THE NONSYMBOLIC NATURE OF GOD AS "IS-NESS" ITSELF

The nonsymbolic nature of God as is-ness itself seems to precede and transcend all other names of God. This concept of is-ness (*isticheit*) is expressed in Japanese as *sono-mama* (そのまま), which "transcends everything, it has no moorings. No concepts can reach it, no understanding can grasp it."[31] Thus, *sono-mama,* that is, "I am that I am," is the most profound statement of the mystery of God. Suzuki correctly points out that "the biblical God is said to have given his name to Moses on Mount Sinai as 'I am that I am.' That is a most profound utterance, for all our religious or spiritual or metaphysical experiences start from it."[32] God as *sono-mama* itself, or is-ness itself, is the most primordial meaning of God that religion or spiritual encounter can experience.

God as is-ness itself is not identical with Tillich's definition of God as "being itself." Both terms are nonsymbolic, but the difference between them is apparent in their differing emphases. The concept of God as is-ness itself stresses the dynamic aspect of God, that is, the essence of the process of change. But the definition of God as being itself emphasizes the structural form of his existence. We must remember that is-ness itself and being itself are not contradictory but complementary. Our attempt to distinguish between these two terms is intended not to prove one of them wrong but to further define the nonsymbolic nature of God.

To compare is-ness itself with being itself, we can begin with Tillich's understanding of the term "being itself" in relation to the unknown God. Tillich is interested in "being" as well as "being itself" from the point of view of ontology: "God as being-itself is the ground of the ontological structure of being without being subject to this structure himself."[33] This does not preclude the dynamic aspect of being, for the structural and dynamic aspect of being are complementary. Thus Tillich makes clear that, since Plato's view of being presupposes the power of being, his own definition of God as "being itself" also presupposes its power.[34] Being comprises both becoming and rest: Becoming is the power and rest is the form. Thus to define God as "being itself" includes both the power of God and the essence of ontological structure.[35]

Tillich wants to maintain the polarity between becoming and rest or between dynamics and form in God, but he is primarily interested in the structural aspect of being.[36] This interest is emphasized in his statements that "God is the ground of the structure of being" and "he *is* the structure."[37] When Robert P. Scharlemann suggested a change from "God as being" to "God is," Tillich's response was unfavorable.[38] Therefore Tillich's definition of God as "being itself" is not totally congruent with the definition of God in Exodus 3:1–15, which emphasizes the verb *is* rather than the ontological structure of being.

THE DYNAMICS OF GOD'S "IS-NESS ITSELF"

Let us review the content of the passage. When Moses asked the name of the God who was revealed to him, God said "I AM WHO I AM." If the passage had ended with this statement, it would be possible to adopt Tillich's definition of God as "being itself." But God clarified his statement by calling himself "YHWH," in order to elucidate his former statement "I AM WHO I AM." Since the name "YHWH" is directly connected with the verb *hayah*, which means "to be" in an active and dynamic sense, the "being" of God in Exodus 3:15 must be differentiated from the "being" of God in the Platonic and Til-lichian sense. "The verb *hayah*, when it refers to God," van Leeuwen said, "expresses his personal, dynamic, active being vis-à-vis his people and his creation."[39] As Boman said, "The *hayah* of God is to act as God, to deal as God, and to carry into effect as God. . . . The *hayah* of God is not given once for all in the great act of Exodus, but is only revealed in that act with particular clarity. Continuously he shows himself in manifestation of grace and mighty acts as the God of Israel."[40]

Here the emphasis is not on the structural aspect of being, as

Tillich would have it, but on the dynamic action of becoming. Moreover the name "YHWH" seems to have its origin in the primitive understanding of lightning and thunder, just as the concept of heaven (*ch'ien*, 乾) in China was directly related to the power of the dragon, which was believed to manifest itself in lightning and thunder.[41] According to van Leeuwen, "The name 'Yahweh,' which is in origin Kenite or Ugaritic, takes us back to an indefinable power encountered in the lightning and thunder."[42] Jacob believes that "Yahweh in its primitive form *yah* was only originally an interjection, a kind of ejaculation uttered in moments of excitement and in connection with the moon cult; the complete name of 'Yahweh,' or 'Yahu' would then be this interjection followed by the personal pronoun for the third person."[43] It seems then reasonable to believe that the name "Yahweh," or "YHWH," which is used in the Old Testament "more than 6,700 times,"[44] is more closely associated with power or energy than with structural existence.

Another commonly used name for God, *El*, "expresses life in its power."[45] As Arend van Leeuwen points out, the meaning of *El*, "God," is associated with the primitive notion of power: "The term *elohim* ["God"] refers to the formless and nameless plurality of primitive forces which make their presence felt in that experience."[46] The literal meaning of the Hebrew words *El* or *Elohim* is "to be strong" or "to be mighty."[47] *El* is associated with the power of creation: "In the beginning God [i.e., *Elohim*] created the heaven and the earth" (Gen. 1:1) Therefore *El*, God, is associated with the power of created phenomena as the mountains of *El* (Ps. 36:7), the cedars of *El* (Ps. 80:11), the stars of *El* (Isa. 14:13), or the army of *Elohim* (1 Chron. 12:22).

Based on the evidence of God's primordial names, we must conclude that the concept of God was in the beginning more closely associated with the idea of power or energy that changes and transforms existence than it was with the formal structure of beings or entities connoted by the Greek word *logos*. "The Hebrew way of conceiving reality" is, as van Leeuwen said, "a changing, moving, affective, and dramatic whole."[48] Thus, to conceive of God as the essential structure of being is at variance with the Hebrew concept of ultimate reality as is-ness itself. God as is-ness itself (*sono-mama*, or "suchness") is primarily the power of change itself. "The principle of Suchness is not static, it is full of dynamic forces."[49]

Since the definition of God's is-ness stresses dynamics rather than the form of being, "becoming itself" seems a better definition of God than "being itself." But becoming itself is not identical with is-ness itself. The idea of becoming, because of its intrinsic limitation, cannot express ultimate reality. I agree with Tillich that "to speak of a 'becoming' God disrupts the balance between dynamics and form and subjects God to a process . . . which is completely open to the future and has the character of an absolute accident. In both cases the divinity of God is undercut."[50] The problem with becoming is, as Tillich points out, its implicit meaning of "not yet," which not only limits the power of God but creates the never-ending process of becoming. Because of its intrinsic limiting "not-yet," becoming cannot be the category of ultimate reality.

If God cannot be "becoming itself" because becoming cannot express the category of the ultimate, we must find a term that can at least suggest this category. If we define becoming as a process of creativity, there must be something that makes this process possible, sustains and provides for it, since becoming is not an expression of the ultimate. In searching for the category of the ultimate that engenders creativity, it is more useful to turn East than West. Even though Spinoza, Bergson, Bradley, and others have dealt with the philosophy of process, the East, as Whitehead points out, has been traditionally oriented toward the metaphysics of process.[51] Out of many eastern metaphysical works I have selected one of the classics of Chinese wisdom literature, the *I ching*, or Book of Changes, to assist in the search for the ultimate category of becoming. The importance of this book cannot be overemphasized.[52] The *I ching* may help us to recognize God as is-ness itself in the category of change, which does not contain the element of "not yet" that limits the category of becoming.

GOD AS CHANGE-ITSELF

We have already seen that becoming, as the process of creativity, falls short of the category of the ultimate. The *I ching* seems to reassure us of this penultimate character of creative becoming. The creative process is possible because of the *i*, or change, which creates and changes everything in the world. Thus becoming, that is, the process of creativity, is a function of change. In the *I ching* the *i*, or change, is the begetter of heaven and earth.[53] Creativity is the characteristic of heaven, while responsiveness is the characteristic of earth. The former is symbolized in the first hexagram, *ch'ien* (乾 , creativity) and the latter in the second hexagram, *k'un* (坤 , responsiveness). The former signifies the infinite concentration of *yang* energy, the latter the infinite concentration of *yin* energy. The hexagram *ch'ien* consists entirely of *yang* (or undivided) lines while the hexagram *k'un* consists entirely of *yin* (or divided) lines. They are complementary to one another and create and recreate everthing in the world. Nothing can exist without them. But these two primordial essences owe their existences to change, which is the ultimate reality of all that is becoming and in process.

ch'ien   k'un

Any process of becoming ultimately results from the interplay of *yin* and *yang* forces. In other words *yin* and *yang* are the basic constituents of becoming. Since these two primary forces are the product of change, change is the source of becoming and the creative process. Thus the Great Commentary to the *I ching* says, "The Great Ultimate (*t'ai chi*, 太極) is in change. Change produces the two primary forms. The two primary forms produce the four images. The four images produce the eight trigrams."[54] "The two primary forms" signify creativity (heaven) and responsiveness (earth), or the prime *yang* and prime *yin*. As the Great

Commentary goes on to say: "Therefore: There are no greater primal images than heaven and earth."[55] By doubling both *yin* and *yang* lines, we get the four images: the old *yang*, new *yin*, old *yin* and new *yang*.[56] By adding another *yin* or *yang* line to the four images or duograms, the eight trigrams are evolved.

According to the *I ching* these eight symbols are the basis for everything in the universe. Here we see the evolution of eight trigrams from the circle of the Great Ultimate, which is identified with change in the Great Commentary of the *I ching*. Fung Yu-lan believes that the diagram of the Great Ultimate (*t'ai chi t'u* 太 極 圖), which was devised by Chou Tun-i (1017–73), "became the first systematic product of Sung and Ming Neo-Confucianism."[57] Furthermore, in his discussion of the Great Ultimate in the *I t'ung* (Explanation of Change) Chou is referring to change.[58] Therefore, Ch'u Chai rightly points out, "the word *I* (or Change) is used interchangeably with the word *Tao*, since *Tao* is life, spontaneity, evolution, or in one word, change itself."[59] It is, then, change, or *tao*, which is also the Great Ultimate, or ultimate reality, that becomes the source of the evolutionary process of becoming.

Just as change is the source of all creative becoming, *tao* is the source of all things. As Lao Tzu says, "The Way [*Tao*] begot one, and the one, two; then the two begot three and three all else."[60] Here the way, or *tao*, is change, which is the source of "one," or creativity (heaven). "Two" refers to heaven and earth, or creativity and responsiveness, which produce three, meaning the trigrams, the basis of hexagrams. Since sixty-four hexagrams constitute the microcosmic symbol of the total universe, everything comes from trigrams. Thus the *Hsi tz'u*, one of the ten "wings" of the *I ching*, says, "One yin and one yang constitute what is called *Tao*."[61] *Tao* is the mother of all things, and "the begetter of all begetting is called the Change."[62] The creative process of becoming finds its ultimate expression in change or *tao*, which is best expressed in the nonsymbolic term "is-ness itself." In other words, is-ness itself, which is known as *tao* as well as (Nirguna) Brahman, nirvana, or YHWH, is also change itself, because *tao* and change are identical. The nonsymbolic statement of is-ness becomes meaningful when it is understood as signifying change. Change not only qualifies the dynamic existence of God's is-ness but also overcomes the "not yet" of creative becoming.

In order to illustrate God's is-ness itself as change itself, let us use a turning wheel as an analogy: God as is-ness occupies the center of this moving wheel and the rest of the wheel represents the universe. This center or axis is the core of the entire wheel, and its motion determines the movements of all of its other parts. This axis, by moving itself, causes the wheel to move and therefore is analogous to change or change itself. It is definitely not the "unmoved mover"; it is the "moving mover," or "changing changer" that is the source of all creative becoming. It is not subject to becoming; it engenders and constitutes the essence of the becoming and changing process. That is why Suzuki referred to the phenomenal world as "the moving images of the eternal essence which alone 'is' and is not subject to becoming."[63]

Change itself is then the most meaningful expression of God's is-ness in the world of constant change and becoming. Everything changes because of change, but change itself is changeless, for it is the "all-changing changeless."[64]

SUMMARY

Let us review the steps of our argument. In order to discover the primordial meaning of God in the Judeo-Christian faith, I have analyzed Exodus 3:1–15, which describes the initial contact between God and Moses. Analysis of "I AM WHO I AM" and "YHWH" has established this God, YHWH, to be incomprehensible, unknowable, and indescribable in any human terms. This God is a reality without attributes and can be described only by his is-ness. The Judeo-Christian God's nonsymbolic nature is identical with Brahman, nirvana, and *tao*. Since ultimate reality, whether called YHWH, Brahman, nirvana, or *tao*, is beyond human qualifications, "is-ness itself" is its only possible definition. Beginning with this initial definition of God's existence as "is-ness itself," I have attempted to find a meaningful metaphysical affirmation of his is-ness itself. To this end I examined Tillich's definition of God as "being itself," which, though it is a nonsymbolic statement about God, does not confront the reality of God's is-ness. Tillich's "being itself" emphasizes the structural form of being rather than the dynamic aspect of God's presence. Therefore I have concluded that to define God as "being itself" is not only contrary to the original, Hebraic definition but inconsistent with God's basic characteristic of is-ness, which is essentially dynamic. The obvious alternative definition of God as "becoming itself" must be rejected because of its intrinsic limitation. The notion of becoming implies "not yet," which violates the perfection and purity of is-ness itself. In eastern philosophy I found a category of the ultimate that accurately describes is-ness—one that comprises being itself and is the source of becoming itself without the limitations and inconsistencies of these categories. According to the *I ching*, change is not only the source of creative becoming but the ultimate reality. Thus the ultimate reality as is-ness can be meaningfully expressed in terms of change itself.

God as change itself is the source of every creative becoming. Like the axis of a moving wheel, change itself changes all parts of the wheel by changing itself. Change, which changes all things, is itself changeless. As the *Tao te ching* says, "Essential nature [*ming*] is everchanging-changeless" (ch. 16). The ultimate reality, then, is the change that is changeless. To understand God's is-ness we have to understand, said Chang Chung-yuan, "the concept of the changeless within the everchanging."[65]

"CHANGE ITSELF" AS CHANGELESS

What is then the real meaning of changelessness if God is change itself? If God is changing reality, does this affect the steadfastness of God in his relations with his people? What becomes of the Hebrew prophets' profound conviction that God is changeless? Malachi says, "I the Lord do not change" (Mal. 3:6). And the Psalmist, agreeing, declares: "They will perish, but thou dost endure; they will all wear out like a garment. Thou changest them like raiment, and they pass away; but thou art the same, and thy years have no end" (Ps. 102:26–27). In the New Testament we find similar affirmations. For example, the Epistle to the Hebrews proclaims that "Jesus Christ is the same yesterday and today and forever" (Heb. 13:8).

If God does not have the characteristic of changelessness, his people cannot trust in him. But we must understand that God's changelessness is not the same as stasis. His changelessness refers to the consistency and steadfastness of his will. In other words, the character of changelessness is a part of the changing reality of God: Changelessness is possible because of change. God is changeless because he is primarily change itself. Changelessness means, then, the changeless pattern of change, or consistent structural change. The changelessness of God does not negate his essential nature as change but affirms the unceasingness of his changing. It is the constancy of change that makes changelessness possible, and therefore the element of changelessness is found within the change itself. "The Taoist would say that the flying arrow represents the changeless within the ever-changing. . . . The arrow moves all the time, but at the same time it does not move at all. To quote the Buddhists: 'Though things move, they are forever motionless; though things are motionless, they do not cease moving.' "[66]

Changelessness is then the constant and regular form of change. "The constancy and regularity of changes are the very essence of the eternal and invariable principle of change."[67] As John Courtney Murray said, "Over against the inconstancy and infidelity of the people, who continually absent themselves from God, the name Yahweh affirms the constancy of God, his unchangeable fidelity to this promise of presence. Malachi, the last of the prophets, stated this first facet of the primitive revelation: 'I [am] Yahweh; I do not change' (3:6.)."[68] Changelessness is primarily God's faithfulness to himself, that is, to "change itself."

If God were not change in the changing world, he would not be in the world. If God were only the "unmoved mover" in the moving universe, he would not be a part of the universe. He would be only an observer, not a participant, in history. But this is not God's role. As Leslie Dewart says: "God does not dip his finger into history; he totally immerses himself in it. When he visits the world he does not come slumming. He comes to stay. He arrives most concretely and decisively of all in the person of the Word in order to make earth and history his home, his permanent residence."[69] If God is concretely in the world of change and transformation, the changing God is more compatible with concrete religious experience than is the absolute, unchanging, and timeless being of traditional theology.[70] The God of unchanging being is not only inconsistent with the changing cosmos but contradicts his own essence as life-giver and life-receiver. God as change itself reaffirms his role as both life-giver and life-receiver. He is the center or the inmost core of the changing world as well as the source of the creative process of becoming. The cosmos is living and changing because of the living and changing God, who is the ground of all things.

It is this vital and dynamic God who is finally responsible for the living and changing universe. As Pittenger says, "The only reasonable explanation of the living cosmos is in fact the living God."[71] To deny the idea of a changing God is to deny the living God, because the living organism is in the process of becoming, which presupposes change. There is no way to separate the world and God. Even the concept of nirvana cannot exist independent of the world of change. "Nirvana is another name for the Emptiness [*Śunyata*],"[72] but it is more than a pure form. It is also "what makes all these things possible; it is a zero full of infinite possibilities, it is a void of inexhaustible contents."[73] Therefore, "Nirvana is samsāra and samsāra is Nirvana."[74] Following the teaching of *Prajñāpāramitā-sūtra,* Suzuki attempts to describe the inseparableness of the infinite from the finite and God's is-ness from our is-ness. He quotes Eckhart's words, "God's is-ness is my is-ness and neither more nor less."[75] God as is-ness itself is inseparable from the world as is-ness. If the world is constantly changing and becoming, as the theory of relativity and nuclear science have suggested, God must be the subject of this change. Therefore our concept of the world predisposes us to believe in a changing God.

God is changeless because he is primarily change itself. God's ever-changing nature incorporates the unchanging patterns of change. Thus God is simultaneously changing and changeless, as Ogden summarizes: "*That* he is ever-changing is itself the product or effect of no change whatever, but is in the strictest sense changeless, the immutable ground of change as such, both his own and others."[76] The God who transcends the distinction between subject and object or between existence and essence is changeless change itself. "The unchanging aspect of *Tao* [or God]," as Donald Munro says, "is compared to the center [*shu* 樞] of a wheel. It is hollow, and hence contains only nothingness (*wu* 無 or *śunyatā*); but its very hollowness allows the wheel to turn on a shaft and thus be effective."[77] God as change itself is, then, eternal change and the heart of change. As Swami Prabhavananda says, "Endless change without, and at the heart of the change an abiding reality—*Brahman.* Endless change within, and at the heart of the change an abiding reality—*Ātman.* . . . *Brahman* and *Ātman* are one and the same. And they summed up the prodigious affirmation in the words *Tat tvam asi*—That thou art."[78] We may also sum up our understanding of the nonsymbolic description of God as change itself or the "heart of change," which is changeless.

Notes

1. Nels F. S. Ferré, *Evil and the Christian Faith* (New York: Harper and Brothers, 1947), p. 75.

2. Thomas Aquinas, *Summa Theologica*, Ia. 9, 1–2.

3. Ibid., Ia. 9, 3.

4. Ibid.

5. Ibid., Ia. 25, 1.

6. Ibid., Ia. 9, 2.

7. See *The Holy Bible: Revised Standard Version Containing Old and New Testaments* (New York: Thomas Nelson and Sons, 1952), p. 58, footnote.

8. The last translation may be closest to the original meaning of the text and is discussed in greater detail elsewhere in this book.

9. See John Courtney Murray, *The Problem of God: Yesterday and Today* (New Haven: Yale University Press, 1964), p. 7.

10. Ibid., p. 13.

11. Edmond Jacob, *Theology of the Old Testament*, trans. Arthur W. Heathcote and Philip J. Allcock (New York: Harper and Brothers, 1958), p. 54.

12. Paul Tillich, *Systematic Theology* (Chicago: University of Chicago Press, 1951), 1: 238.

13. See footnote "f," *The Holy Bible: Revised Standard Version*, p. 58.

14. Paul Tillich's definition of God as "being-itself" is also a nonsymbolic statement, but it is inadequate.

15. *Kena* 3.

16. *Katha* 6:12.

17. See the argument in Edward Conze, *Buddhism: Its Essence and Development* (Oxford: Bruno Cassirer, 1951), pp. 38–43.

18. *Samyutta-nikāya* IV, 251–52.

19. Huston Smith, *The Religions of Man* (New York: Harper & Brothers, 1958), p. 125.

20. *Udāna* 80.

21. Quoted in Edward Conze, ed., *Buddhist Texts Through the Ages* (Oxford: Bruno Cassirer, 1954), pp. 99–100.

22. Smith, *The Religions of Man*, p. 360, footnote 30.

23. Conze, *Buddhism*, p. 134.

24. Chang Chung-yuan, *Creativity and Taoism* (New York: Harper and Row, 1970), p. 30.

25. Confucians also use the term *tao*, but to embody a very different set of meanings. For Confucius "it has a more moralistic than metaphysical

connotation" (D. T. Suzuki, *Mysticism: Christian and Buddhist*. New York: Harper and Row, 1957, p. 20).

26. Ibid.

27. *Tao te ching*, ch. 14.

28. Ibid., ch. 4.

29. Suzuki, *Mysticism*, pp. 18–19.

30. *Tao te ching*, ch. 25.

31. Suzuki, *Mysticism*, pp. 76–77.

32. Ibid., p. 126.

33. Paul Tillich, *Systematic Theology* (Chicago: University of Chicago Press, 1951), 1: 239.

34. Ibid., p. 236.

35. Ibid., p. 247.

36. Ibid.

37. Ibid., p. 239.

38. See Robert P. Scharlemann, "Tillich's Method of Correlation: Two Proposed Revisions," *Journal of Religion* 46 (January 1966): 92ff; and Paul Tillich, "Rejoinder," in the same issue, pp. 184ff.

39. Arend T. van Leeuwen, *Christianity in World History*, trans. H. H. Hoskins (New York: Charles Scribner's Sons, 1964), p. 47.

40. Thorleif Boman, *Hebrew Thought Compared with Greek*, trans. Jules L. Moreau (Philadelphia: Westminster Press, 1960), p. 47.

41. See the first hexagram of the *I ching*.

42. Van Leeuwen, *Christianity in World History*, p. 51.

43. Jacob, *Theology of the Old Testament*, p. 48.

44. Ludwig Koehler, *Old Testament Theology*, trans. A. S. Todd (Philadelphia: Westminster Press, 1957), p. 41.

45. Jacob, *Theology of the Old Testament*, p. 51.

46. Van Leeuwen, *Christianity in World History*, p. 51.

47. Alan Richardson, *A Theological Word Book of the Bible* (New York: Macmillan, 1950), p. 91.

48. Van Leeuwen, *Christianity in World History*, p. 47.

49. Suzuki, *Mysticism*, p. 82.

50. Tillich, *Systematic Theology*, 1:247.

51. Alfred North Whitehead, *Process and Reality: An Essay in Cosmology* (New York: Macmillan Company, 1929), p. 11.

52. For the authorship of the *I ching*, see J. Y. Lee, "Some Reflections on the Authorship of the *I ching*," *Numen* 17 (December 1970), 200–10; for the impact of the *I ching* on later Chinese philosophies see J. Y. Lee, *The Principle of Changes: Understanding the I Ching* (New Hyde Park, New York: University Books, 1971), pp. 40ff.

53. *Ta Chuan,* sec. I, ch. 5.

54. Ibid., sec. I, ch. 11. See also Introduction.

55. Ibid.

56. For comprehensive illustrations see J. Y. Lee, *The Principle of Changes,* pp. 48, 117ff.

57. Fung Yu-lan, *A History of Chinese Philosophy* (Princeton: Princeton University Press, 1953), 2:442.

58. Ibid.

59. Ch'u Chai and Winberg Chai, ed., *I Ching: Book of Changes,* trans. by James Legge (New Hyde Park, New York: University Books, 1964), pp. xl–xli.

60. *Tao te ching,* ch. 42.

61. Sec. I, ch. 5.

62. *Ta chuan,* sec. I, ch. 5.

63. Suzuki, *Mysticism,* p. 106.

64. Chang Chung-yuan interprets the word *"ch'ang,"* which is one of the basic concepts of Taoism, as the "all-changing changeless" (*Creativity and Taoism,* New York: Julian Press, 1963, p. 127).

65. Ibid., p. 72.

66. Ibid.

67. Lee, *The Principle of Changes,* p. 64.

68. Murray, *The Problem of God,* p. 11.

69. Leslie Dewart, *The Future of Belief: Theism in a World Come of Age* (New York: Herder and Herder, 1965), p. 194.

70. Thomas W. Ogletree, "A Christological Assessment of Dipolar Theism," *Journal of Religion* 49 (1967):92.

71. Norman Pittenger, "A Contemporary Trend in North American Theology: Process Thought and Christian Faith," *Religion in Life* 34 (1965):502.

72. D. T. Suzuki, *On Indian Mahayana Buddhism,* ed. Edward Conze (New York: Harper and Row, 1968), p. 270.

73. Ibid.

74. *The Heart Sutra,* III, 9–14; Suzuki, *Mysticism,* p. 110.

75. Suzuki, ibid., p. 120.

76. Schubert Ogden, *The Reality of God and Other Essays* (New York: Harper and Row, 1966), p. 60.

77. Donald Munro, *The Concept of Man in Early China* (Stanford: Stanford University Press, 1969), p. 128.

78. Swami Prabhavananda, *The Spiritual Heritage of India* (Hollywood: Vedanta Press, 1963), p. 55.

CHAPTER III

BOTH-AND AS ULTIMATE REALITY: GOD AS INCLUSIVENESS

Change itself as the ultimate reality always manifests itself in a dipolar process, because change generates two: *yin* and *yang*. Since *yin* and *yang* are inherent in all things, they are the primordial categories of our thinking, which, because it must include both, is necessarily a "both-and" way of thinking. Because of its dipolar manifestation, the ultimate reality can be conceived only by "both-and" thinking. "Both-and" thinking proves to be consistent with most of God's attributes in the Judeo-Christian tradition. For example, the transcendence and immanence of the divine nature coexist. We cannot say that God is *either* transcendent *or* immanent. The God of Judeo-Christian faith is at the same time *both* transcendent *and* immanent. If God were transcendent only, there would be no way for God to communicate with us. If God were immanent only, God would not be divine. Just as *yin* is inseparable from *yang*, God's immanence is one with God's transcendence. That is why Bonhoeffer can say, "The transcendent is not infinitely remote, but close at hand."[1] Because divine nature is expressed in a "both-and," divine immanence incorporates divine transcendence, and divine transcendence incorporates divine immanence. In order to be known to us, God must be both transcendent and immanent simultaneously. God is likewise both holy and loving, both judging and forgiving, both revealed and hidden.

GOD AS BOTH PERSONAL AND IMPERSONAL

Nevertheless some attributes applied by Judeo-Christian teachings to the divine nature seem not to lend themselves to "both-and" description; we do not feel that the antitheses of these attributes are also applicable to the Judeo-Christian God. For example, the God of Judeo-Christian faith is commonly thought of as a personal God; we do not think of people worshipping an impersonal being. Furthermore we feel that, to be divine, God must also be good. God, according to the Christian tradition, cannot encompass the antithesis of personal or the antithesis of absolute good. The idea of a personal God is directly related to the ecological problem, and the idea of God's goodness to the problem of theodicy, which asks how evil can exist in the world if God is good. Let us examine these two problems in relation to the "both-and" way of thinking.

According to the "both-and" way of thinking God cannot be *either* personal *or* impersonal. God must be *both* personal *and* impersonal. In other words the personal God is also the impersonal God. Let us clarify what we mean by *personal* and *impersonal*. For our working definition, let us define *personal* as having the nature of a person. Thus the personal God is the God who bears the nature of a person, who is different from animals, plants, and other nonhuman organisms. *Impersonal* is the antithesis of personal. The impersonal God does not have the nature of a person. The importance of the personal God for Christianity is evident in the credal definition of the trinitarian God as three Persons. Because God bears the nature of a person, God is also called by the personal pronoun *he*. Christians find it unacceptable to call God by the impersonal pronoun *it*. Moreover God is called by the masculine personal pronoun; in Judeo-Christian tradition God is never called *she*. Therefore gender is a part of our Judeo-Christian concept of a personal God.

GOD AS BOTH MALE AND FEMALE

The women's liberation movement has forced the question of the divine gender upon our attention. Must God be male? Can

God also be female? In the Scriptures God bears symbols or names that are typically masculine, for example, Heavenly Father or Son of God. In essence God transcends all such symbolic expressions as well as distinction of gender. God's identification with the masculine gender is the result solely of the social conditions in which the Scriptures originated. In other words, God became "he" because Judeo-Christian society was patriarchal. Had the society in which our concept of God originated been matriarchal, we would think of God as feminine. The Taoist tradition provides evidence for this. In the writings of Lao Tzu, *tao* is symbolized by the "mother" instead of "father," emptiness instead of fullness, weakness instead of strength, valley instead of peak, and womb instead of phallus. Clearly, then, the gender attributed to divinity is determined by the social orientation of the worshipper. In essence God is the source of all, both male and female.

Since God is at once transcendent and immanent, God is not only the negation of all genders but also the affirmation of all genders. Therefore God must be both male and female and at the same time neither male nor female. Since the ultimate reality is known only in manifestation, that is, in immanence, God is known as both male and female. Indian *deva-śakti* images, which to uninformed westerners may seem lewd, are simply iconographic expressions of the simultaneous maleness and femaleness of divinity. The Indian people find it natural to think in "both-and" terms. As Heimann says, "The West thinks in *aut-aut*, the disjunctive 'either-or' "; India, on the other hand, visualizes a "continuous stream of interrelated moments of *sive-sive*, the 'this as well as that' in an endless series of changes and transformations."[2]

Moreover in most archaic religions the supreme or divine beings were regarded as androgyne and as simultaneously heavenly and earthly. Androgyny, as sexual completeness, symbolizes the perfection of being. According to Eliade, "Androgyny has become a general formula signifying *autonomy, strength, wholeness*; to say of a divinity that it is androgyne is as much as to say that it is the ultimate being, the ultimate reality."[3] An androgynous divinity is more nearly the ultimate reality than a purely male or female divinity. But it would be misleading to call the God of Christianity androgynous, because God transcends the category of gender. The God of Christianity is best expressed as comprising both male and female as well as neither male nor female. This kind of divine nature, which is totally inclusive as well as totally exclusive, can be characterized by the godhead, which resembles the Upanishadic symbol *IT*, the symbol of *sive-sive*.[4] *It* is not only the inclusive symbol of *sive-sive* but also the exclusive symbol of *neti-neti*, "neither this nor that." Perhaps that is why the Upanishads call ultimate reality, Brahman, by the neuter pronoun *it* rather than *he* or *she*.

In describing the divine nature we must understand that God is simultaneously both he and she as well as neither he nor she. The use of the neuter pronoun *it* for the divine may provide not only a solution to the descriptive problem of divine gender but also a description of God in terms of change that manifests itself in both personal and impersonal categories. It is not my purpose to challenge the Judeo-Christian tradition of referring to God as "he" but only to point out that God, even when called "he," is more than merely masculine.

PROBLEMS AND LIMITATIONS OF A PERSONAL GOD

Let us return to the Christian concept of personal God. As we have indicated, westerners conventionally think of the divine nature as masculine because the society in which the Judeo-Christian tradition originated was patriarchal. It may well be that westerners think of the divine nature as personal because of their view of the human condition and the human place in the cosmos. As illustrations, let us compare the Chinese Confucian idea of ultimate reality with the Chinese Taoist idea of ultimate reality. Both Confucians and Taoists call ultimate reality *tao*, but they mean very different things by the word. The Confucian *tao* is the supreme principle of human, societal existence, encompassing what we would consider both morals and manners and religious rituals. The Master (Confucius) said, "*Tao* is not far from man. If what one takes to be *tao* is far from man, it cannot be considered the true *tao*."[5] For Confucians, *tao* means right personal relationships. Ku Hung-ming comments that the *tao* in man is closely related to the Christian notion of "the kingdom of God within you."[6] In other words, the Confucian's understanding of *tao* is almost identical with the Christian idea of God.

Taoists, on the other hand, regard *tao* as a cosmic rather than human principle. Lao Tzu, the founder of Taoism, needing somehow to express the inexpressible, resorts solely to impersonal symbols. Tao is compared to "rivers and streams running into the sea,"[7] "water,"[8] "the valley,"[9] "an empty bowl,"[10] and "the door."[11] For Taoists, *tao* is the principle of the whole natural cosmos, of which human life and community are a harmonious but infinitely insignificant part. It is the Taoist concern with cosmic process that shaped the concept of an impersonal *tao*; the Confucian preoccupation with social harmony shaped the concept of a more personal *tao*. Chinese life, however, has been singularly free from the passion for religious or philosophical exclusivity that has afflicted the West, and most Chinese have managed to be simultaneously and comfortably Confucian and Taoist. Just as their concept of *tao* has encompassed both the personal and the utterly impersonal, so too they have conceived of *t'ien* (天 , "heaven") simultaneously as the impersonal sky and as the utterly personalized King of Kings, Shang Ti. It is a range of meanings familiar to westerners, for whom "heaven" can be literally "the sky" or symbolically "God" (as in such expressions as "Heaven only knows!" or "Heaven forbid!").

Like *tao* and heaven, ultimate reality can be conceived of either personally or impersonally—or both personally and impersonally, depending on a people's ethos. The ultimate reality that Christians have traditionally believed in is predominantly but not wholly personal. The reality of God is called *Logos*, or *word*, in the Old Testament as well as in the Fourth Gospel of the New Testament, and *Logos* as a metaphysical symbol is certainly more impersonal than personal. Moreover, Yahweh and Elohim, the ancient Hebrew names of God, originally designated impersonal, natural forces, which were later personified and given other and more personal names. As Arend van Leeuwen says, "The name 'Yahweh,' which is in origin Kenite or Ugaritic, takes us back to an indefinable power encountered in the lightning and thunder. The term *elohim* ["God"] refers to the formless and nameless plurality of primitive forces which make their presence felt in that experience."[12] They were closely identified with impersonal and natural objects that possessed the power of change, such as lightning, thunder, mountains, and rivers. When the people of Israel sought political independence, they personified their God by calling him King, Lord, and Master.

How and why did the originally impersonal Judeo-Christian concept of God become personalized? The primordial name of God in the Old Testament, YHWH, found in Exodus 3:1–15, is related to the verb "to be" or to the noun "is-ness." This affirmation of God as is-ness itself seems to transcend the distinction between personal and impersonal being, but YHWH later came to be thought of as a personal being. Let us see how the transition from impersonal or nonpersonal God occurred in Israelite history.

When the Judaic faith begins to expand—from Moses' first sight of the burning bush to the triumphant conclusion of the Exodus—God comes to be thought of as a personal emancipator. He becomes first a powerful magician who terrifies pharaoh and finally breaks his resistance, then the Hebrews' leader to the promised land. There he becomes first the warrior-king who leads their successful fight against the indigenes and finally legislator-king ruling over their newly established nation.

In the New Testament the kingdom of God is described in moral and ethical terms, and God is described in terms of political or social dominance—as Father, Master, Lord. God became personal, then, in part because of historical circumstances. But it is also possible that because we are persons we cannot easily conceive of any but a personal God. Easy or not, however, we must think of God as more than personal. God is "an expansive force which impels persons to go out from and beyond themselves."[13] To conceive of God as purely personal is to limit him and eventually to create a dichotomy between personal and impersonal beings.

The tragic consequence of conceiving of God solely as personal is our erroneous belief that there is a qualitative distinction between personal and impersonal beings, between man and nature, and that impersonal beings are excluded from divine providence. Traditional Christianity asserts that the image of God makes people different from nature and closer to the divine, but traditional Christianity has misunderstood the image of God in people, and with this misunderstanding the ecological crisis began. The image of God or likeness of God must not be understood as the analogy of being but as the analogy of relation.[14] It is not something *in* persons; it is the relationship between God and persons. In other words, what makes persons different from other beings is not their ontic nature but the function of their relationship with God. In this sense humankind is ontologically identical with nature but functionally different from it.

This idea is clearly expressed in the trigrams of the *I ching.* In the trigrams the central line signifies person, the upper line heaven (*yang*), and the lower line earth (*yin*). The trigram is the combination of broken lines (*yin*), signifying earth, with unbroken lines (*yang*), signifying heaven. Therefore, the person, who occupies the center, is the product of both of them. In other words, persons are part of heaven and earth, or *yang* and *yin*. There is no ontic uniqueness in persons. But persons do have a functional uniqueness, for they occupy the center, the mediating position between heaven and earth.

Likewise the image of God in persons is functional. People and nature, personal and impersonal beings, are essentially identical. God is present not only in persons but in all animals. He is the God of persons, of trees, of stones, of everything that exists in the world. Jesus said it: "Look at the birds of the air: they neither sow nor reap nor gather into barns, and yet your heavenly Father feeds them" (Matt. 6:26). And "Consider the lilies of the field, how they grow; they neither toil nor spin; yet I tell you, even Solomon in all his glory was not arrayed like one of these. But if God so clothes the grass of the field, which today is alive and tomorrow is thrown into the oven, will he not much more clothe you, O men of little faith?" (Matt. 6:28–30). It is God who makes grass grow and decay just as he makes people to be born and die. God is in all things, because he is the change that changes all things by growth and decay or by expansion and contraction. Since God is the change that engenders every process of becoming, God must be the inner source of everything in the world.

This idea of God is expressed in the Upanishads as Ātman, the inner self (soul) of every individual entity, which is identical with Brahman, the true self of the cosmos. It is believed that one of the greatest insights contained in the Upanishads is the so-called Brahman/Ātman synthesis, that is, the identification of the individual self (soul) with the universal self (soul). But this is an oversimplification, since Ātman means more than the individual soul. Ātman is the soul of the all and is therefore merely another word for Brahman.[15] Ātman as the ultimate reality dwells in all things, whether they are personal or impersonal in nature. It is then best defined as the ground of all things. The Ātman is in people, in the earth, in the body, in the waters, in speech, in wind, in breath, in the sun, in the ear, in the mind, in lightning, in thunder, and in space. All these are just Ātman.[16] The dialogue between Ushasta Cākrayāna and Yāynavalkya portrays Ātman/ Brahman as the ground of all things:

Ushasta Cākrāyana said: "This has been explained to me just as one might say, 'This is a cow. This is a horse.' Explain to me him who is just the Brahma present and not beyond our ken, him who is the Soul in all things."
    "He is your soul, which is in all things."
    "Which one, O Yājnavalkya, is in all things?"
    "You could not see the seer of seeing. You could not hear the hearer of hearing. You could not think the thinker of thinking. You could not understand the understander of understanding. He is your soul, which is in all things. Aught else than Him [or, than this] is wretched."[17]

If we believe, following Tillich's definition, that God is the ground of all things, then he is equivalent to Ātman in the Upanishads. That kind of God certainly transcends the traditional concept of a personal God, for he is the God of all things, personal and impersonal. Following Upanishadic philosophy, we can say that God is greater than the greatest and smaller than the smallest of our understanding. He is beyond this world and at the same time within this world.[18] Thus God is total: He is totally inclusive and totally exclusive; he is wholly transcendent and wholly immanent; he is wholly personal and wholly impersonal. He is "both-and."

PROBLEMS OF GOD AND EVIL

This brings us to the question of God's relationship to good and evil. One of the essential qualities of the Judeo-Christian concept of God is goodness. It is almost unthinkable in the Judeo-Christian tradition that God should partake of evil. In the past, the total goodness of God has been accepted almost without question. But if God is inclusive, if the divine nature is "both-and" does that not mean that God includes evil? Can the all-powerful and good God cause or countenance the evils of the world? This question is theodicy: the attempt to account for the palpable evil in the world without denying or limiting the good-ness of God. But the problem of evil lies not with the nature of God but with our way of thinking.

If we believe that God's absoluteness lies in his inclusion of all aspects of the world, and if we admit the existence of evil, then we must grant that God includes the existence of evil. God must be both good and evil. If he were not, we would be forced to posit that evil exists independently of God and in conflict with him.

Let us examine first biblical and then present-day concepts of demonic power. The earliest parts of the Old Testament are monistic; only later did a foreign dualism, in which the god of good is in conflict with the god of evil, enter the Judaic tradition. "Through the Babylonian and Persian influence, the concept of cosmic dualism began to permeate the life of the people of Israel at the later Old Testament period."[19] The Babylonian and Persian cults, without refuting the Judeo-Christian account of original creation, modified the original Old Testament monism into a dualistic worldview of opposed good and evil.[20] That dualistic view found vivid expression in such apocalyptic writings as Daniel, Enoch, and Ezra. There we find the conflict between good and evil, between the old age and the new, between the old creation and the new.

The dualistic worldview persists in the New Testament. The power of evil is manifest in the figure of Satan, who tempted Jesus in the wilderness, and in the demonic spirits whom Jesus later cast out from the sick, thereby releasing them from the power of evil. In general, "the demons in the Synoptic Gospels are more the putative cause of afflictions which came to individuals, whereas the cosmic powers in Paul's Epistles are . . . more impersonal . . . forces."[21] To Paul, God and evil were at war in the cosmos, and Christ was the victor and the agent of human victory over the cosmic powers of evil: "Thanks be to God, who give us the victory through our Lord Jesus Christ" (1 Cor. 15:57). It is this concept of cosmic dualism that leads Paul to differentiate explicitly, much as the apocalyptic writers had done, between the old creation and the new (2 Cor. 5:17). Paul predicts the imminent end of the old world and the dawning of the new through the death of Christ. As Richardson says, "The death of Christ has reconciled to God the hostile, fallen powers, and set free from bondage not only humanity but the world powers as well; redemption also had been upon a cosmic scale."[22] Aulén points out that this objective character of Christ's triumph over the cosmic powers of evil continued to be a favorite theme of even the subapostolic writers.[23] But is the idea of cosmic dualism valid for us?

The idea of demonic power as the source of evil in the world entered Jewish apocalyptic and Gnostic redemption myths from Zoroastrianism and was perpetuated in the later Old Testament and in the New Testament. To demythologize New Testament cosmology, then, as Bultmann suggests,[24] is in fact to de-demonologize it.[25] To demythologize the New Testament is to realize that the conflict between God and evil, which New Testament authors considered an ultimate reality, was merely a human, historically limited interpretation of the life of their times. Furthermore, this dualistic conflict between good and evil contradicts the view that the world was created from nothing, that everything, whether good or evil, comes from God, the ultimate reality. Absolute monotheism is incompatible with any kind of dualism, including the dualism of God and evil. There cannot be any conflict between evil and God, because everything comes from God and what is from God is good.

Eliminating the dualistic worldview seems to solve the problem of evil. But as Bultmann suggests, the real problem is not faulty cosmology but erroneous definition of the problem of evil.

The problem is existential, but it was expressed in the New Testament through cosmic imagery and on a cosmic scale as an ultimate conflict between God and demonic power. Evil, however, is not an ultimate problem of God but an existential problem of humanity. Evil is existential, not essential, because it became real in humanity's transition from essence to existence. It is in humanity's existence, that is, in our Fall, that we experience the problem of good and evil. Before our Fall good and evil were not a problem, because they complemented each other. Only after the Fall were they dichotomized and in conflict. According to Genesis our knowledge of the dichotomy between good and evil came about when Adam ate the fruit of the tree (Gen. 3:22). Before that time, as Bonhoeffer says, "Adam knows neither what is good nor what is evil; in the most particular sense he lives beyond good and evil."[26]

Therefore evil is existential, a problem resulting from humanity's *ex*-istence, or the distortion of our essential being. Because of evil's existential nature, it cannot be *ultimately* in conflict with God. We are conditioned by Aristotelian logic—the logic of "either-or"—to think that God must be *either* good *or* evil. In this kind of absolute classification, good God cannot be evil. Evil, which is existential, we erroneously conceive to be irreconcilable with the existence of God, ultimate reality. But the evil we experience in life does not exist in the same dimension, or category, as God.

If evil is an existential problem, good is also existential. Conditions are good or evil relative to our existential situations. This idea is perfectly illustrated by the Taoist story about a farmer whose horse ran away. His neighbor commiserated with him, saying, "Who knows what's good or bad?" The next day the horse returned, bringing wild horses with it. This time the neighbor congratulated him, again saying, "Who knows what's good or bad?" On the following day the farmer's son tried to mount one of the wild horses and fell off, breaking his leg. Again the neighbor offered commiseration: "Who knows what's good or bad?" The following day soldiers came to town to draft the young men into the army. Because of his injury the son was not drafted.[27]

Good and evil are conditional; there is no intrinsic difference between them. They cannot be absolute because they are relative. Thus good and evil cannot be categorized in "either-or" logic. That is why God, who is absolute, is not subject to this kind of categorization. We cannot say that God is absolutely good, because that eliminates the possibility of evil altogether. We can, however, say that God is more than good, because he transcends our category of good. Likewise God is more than evil, because he transcends the category of evil. Good and evil are not dual, conflicting, ultimate realities; they are both subsumed in the ultimate reality. If God is inclusive of all things, he is certainly the source of good and evil. Because they are part of process, they are not in conflict but complement each other; they make the whole possible.

In that respect evil is not the enemy of good but its necessary counterpart. Evil and good are not different essences but differing existential manifestations of human situations. They can be distinguished only in actual human situations. Furthermore they are mutually interdependent. In an ultimate sense what is good is also evil and what is evil is also good. This interdependence is based on a relativistic worldview that acknowledges nothing fixed or stationary, including moral and ethical decisions. "From the transcendental viewpoint, good and evil are, on the contrary, as illusory and relative as all other pairs of opposites: hot-cold, agreeable-disagreeable, long-short, visible-invisible, etc."[28] They are phenomenally differentiated but ultimately inseparable. Good and evil are like waves on water: The waves move, but they are a surface phenomenon; they do not affect the water below.

Lao Tzu explains the necessary complementarity and the relativity of good and evil: "Surely the good man is the bad man's teacher; and the bad man is the good man's business. If the one does not respect his teacher, or the other does not love his business, his error is very great."[29] Later he says, "Bad fortune will promote the good. Good fortune, too, gives rise to bad."[30] In terms of the totality of existence one's good is another's evil: Roast duck is good, but not for the duck. The contemporary civilized world enjoys a hitherto unequalled level of well-being, achieved by means of scientific technology but, at the expense of, that is, *by doing evil to*, animal and plant life, earth, air, and water. The world is an organic whole, and from this point of view our every "progress" is also a retrogression, our every amelioration is simultaneously an impairment.

Thus the ultimate reality, whose nature simultaneously includes and excludes everything, is not subject to the phenomenal distinction between good and evil. That does not mean that God is indifferent to the problem of evil. He transcends the distinction between good and evil but is a part of the struggle between them. If God acknowledges the problem, what is his solution? Will he eliminate evil from the existential situation completely?

According to the exclusive way of thinking, the solution to the problem of evil is to eliminate evil completely from the world. Because New Testament cosmology reflects the dualistic worldview of Jewish apocalyptic and Gnostic redemptive myths, the New Testament interprets Jesus' victory over the power of evil as the solution to the problem of evil. But that kind of solution presupposes absolute dualism, that is, the coequality of God and the Devil,[31] which is alien to the Judeo-Christian worldview. God, in Judeo-Christian belief, is the ultimate reality by whose sole creativity all things come to be. In other words, the Hebrew worldview is monistic. It contains no concept of co-ultimate realities. The Satan figures that appear in the Old and New Testaments are not God's equals but merely divine creatures like the angels. They cannot be complements of the ultimate. Since good and evil are existential complements, the elimination of evil would also eliminate good. Thus elimination is not a valid solution to the problem of evil. God deals with the problem of evil by enabling reversion from it to its polar opposite—good.

Jesus was aware of the relativity of moral goodness and evil. He condemned those who distinguished absolutely between good and evil. The Pharisees were typical of those who so distinguished, thereby creating moral idols. Jesus knew that good and evil are not ultimately in conflict, for their distinction is phenomenal or existential. God, for Jesus, transcended any categorical distinction, because he is the source and ground of all things, whether good or evil. Good and evil are complementary elements of the ultimate wholeness of creation. That is why Jesus attempted to avoid pitting one against the other. Jesus understood the principle of change, according to which what has expanded to its maximum degree must revert to its opposite. In other words when good reaches its maximum intensity, it will revert to evil.

Let us take the core of Jesus' teaching, the Sermon on the Mount: "Blessed are you poor, for yours is the kingdom of God. Blessed are you that hunger now, for you shall be satisfied. Blessed are you that weep now, for you shall laugh. Blessed are you when men hate you. . . . But woe to you that are rich, for you have received your consolation. Woe to you that are full now, for you shall hunger . . . " (Luke 6:21ff.). Clearly the Sermon on the Mount is saying that every condition upon reaching its maximum will revert to its opposite. It presupposes the existence of pairs of opposites in all things. That is why Jesus said, "Do good to those who hate you, bless those who curse you, pray for those who abuse you" (Luke 6:27–28). Jesus knew the necessary complementarity of opposites, and that is why he said, "If any one would be first, he must be last of all and servant of all" (Mark 9:35), or "For whoever would save his life will lose it, and whoever loses his life for my sake will find it" (Matt. 16:35), or "He who is greatest among you shall be your servant; whoever exalts himself will be humbled, and whoever humbles himself will be exalted" (Matt. 23:11–12).

These passages show us that the polarities they contain are not conflicting but complementary, and that intrinsic to each is its reversion to the other. Inherent in the extreme of evil is its reversion to good. That is why Jesus taught that evil must be overcome with good. Good and evil are relative, and both necessary to the creative existence of the world. Jesus did not suggest solving the problem of evil by eliminating it but by reverting from it, for evil presupposes good. Reversion as the solution of the problem is well illustrated by a Zen *koan* (intellectual puzzle). A Zen master said, "If you have a staff, I shall give you one; if you do not have a staff, I will take one away from you."[32] Even Luther asserts the coexistence of good and evil, or salvation and sin, in the famous phrase *simul iustus et peccator,* meaning literally that humanity is simultaneously sinful and justified, rendered incapable of perfection by inherent evil and incapable of evil by inherent goodness.

Good and evil are, as we have indicated, not ontic realities but relational, phenomenal manifestations of the ultimate reality, which is the process of change. To be in harmony with this changing process is good, to be in disharmony with it is evil. To be good means to be in accord with the way of change, which is equivalent to saying that justification (or righteousness) is to be in accord with the divine. To be evil means to be in disharmony with the process of change. Thus the criterion of good is not its identification with the divine nature, or process of change, but its harmony with it. It is the principle of harmony or disharmony which decides the nature of good and evil. The ultimate reality transcends good and evil and the distinction between them, but it includes both, and harmony or disharmony with ultimate reality determines what is existentially good or evil.

That is how God, as the ultimate reality, participates in the relation between evil and good, even though his essential nature transcends it. Jesus seems to have preached that kind of God, but the cosmic dualism of his time distorted his image of the ultimate. That cosmic dualism makes the New Testament appear to say that God is fighting against the demonic power. If we strip off the dualism, which is an alien element in the New Testament, the power of evil is seen to belong in the domain of the ultimate reality. It is not a problem to reconcile God with existential evil, except when God is falsely conceived of as the obverse of a cosmic duality whose reverse is evil. It was the dualistic way of thinking, that is, "either-or" thinking that created good and evil as the problem of God. In the inclusive, or *yin-yang*, way of thinking, good and evil are not in conflict but are complementary polarities in the creative process of change.

If we define the ultimate reality as the source and ground of everything that is or is to become, it includes everything that is or is to become. Its inclusiveness is inherent in its transcendence of any finite categorization. Thus it is unknowable, indescribable, ineffable, yet it is the ground of all that we know and experience.

God is a *mysterium tremendum,* yet is also *fascinans.* Meister Eckhart sought to express the idea of transcendence in the phrase "God is nearer to me than I am to my own self." Carl Michalson says, "Transcendence does not jeopardize the intention of immanence, which is simply to articulate the nearness of God."[33] Transcendence and immanence complement each other. The divine transcendence is possible in its immanence, and its immanence is possible in its transcendence. One cannot exist without the other. This divine paradox, this "both-and," is beyond our rational and logical categorization. Even the sum of all great names such as Lord, Master, Heavenly Father, King, and Savior cannot approach the greatness and ineffableness of God.

We can express God as *neti, neti* ("neither this nor that") because God is ineffable, but the category of "neither-nor" must be complemented by the category of "both-and." Even though the ultimate reality cannot be contained even in our most sophisticated formulations, "this acknowledgement is not," as Schilling said, "an invitation to stop thinking, but rather a summons to use our God-given capacities to understand as fully as possible."[34] Therefore our approach to the understanding of the ultimate reality must be the most inclusive category of thinking, that is, "both-and," which always connotes its complement "neither-nor." As Nels Ferré has remarked, "There is here no place for paradox, excluded middle, *totum simul* or *Alles auf einmal.* What we need is a contrapetal ontology or theology expressible only in terms of contrapetal logic."[35] This "contrapetal" logic, that is, the logic of complementing contradictions, is the "both-and" way of thinking, which the Chinese express by the concepts *yin* and *yang.*[36] This "both-and" way of thinking forces us to conclude that God in his immanence is simultaneously personal and impersonal, good and evil. But God in his transcendence is neither personal nor impersonal, neither good nor evil, because in addition to "both-and" he is "neither-nor."

It is encouraging to see the use of the category of "both-and" in contemporary theology. Ogden, for example, thinks that "the new theism, then, requires a philosophy that can represent God as both 'supremely relative and supremely absolute.' "[37] He sees "both-and" as a way of thinking that can comprehend the most inclusive reality of God. We must not forget, however, that the divine category of "both-and" is possible because of the divine category of "neither-nor." Without the latter God could not transcend the world.

Notes

1. Dietrich Bonhoeffer, *Prisoner for God: Letters and Papers from Prison* (New York: Macmillan, 1954), p. 175.

2. Betty Heimann, *Facets of Indian Thought* (London: Allen and Unwin, 1964), p. 168.

3. Mircea Eliade, *Myths, Dreams, and Mysteries,* trans. Philip Mairet (New York: Harper Torchbook, 1967), p. 175.

4. Heimann, *Facets of Indian Thought,* p. 168.

5. *Chung Yung,* XIII, 1.

6. Ku Hung-ming, trans., *The Conduct of Life* (Taipei, 1956), p. 25 (privately published).

7. *Tao te ching*, 32, 66.

8. Ibid., 8.

9. Ibid., 6.

10. Ibid., 4.

11. Ibid., 1.

12. Arend van Leeuwen, *Christianity in World History: The Meeting of the Faiths of East and West,* trans. H. H. Hoskins (New York: Charles Scribner's Sons, 1964), p. 51.

13. Leslie Dewart, *The Future of Belief: Theism in a World Come of Age* (New York: Herder and Herder, 1966), p. 189.

14. It was Dietrich Bonhoeffer who suggested the *imago Dei* as the *analogia relationis* in his *Creation and Fall.* This idea was taken up by Karl Barth and expounded in his *Church Dogmatics.* See J. Y. Lee, "Karl Barth's Use of Analogy in His *Church Dogmatics,"* *Scottish Journal of Theology,* June 1969, pp. 42–43.

15. R. C. Zaehner, *Hinduism* (London: Oxford University Press, 1962), p. 49.

16. *Brihad-Aranyaka Upanishad,* II, 5 (trans. Robert E. Hume).

17. Ibid., III, 4, 2 (trans. Robert E. Hume).

18. Heimann, *Facets of Indian Thought,* pp. 123–24.

19. J. Y. Lee, "Interpreting the Demonic Powers in Pauline Thought," *Novum Testamentum* 12 (fasc. 1, 1970):57.

20. Rudolf Bultmann, *Primitive Christianity in Its Contemporary Setting* (New York: Meridian Books, 1959), p. 82.

21. J. Y. Lee, "Interpreting the Demonic Powers in Pauline Thought," p. 55.

22. Alan Richardson, *An Introduction to the Theology of the New Testament* (New York: Harper and Brothers, 1958), p. 213.

23. Gustaf Aulén, *Christus Victor: An Historical Study of the Three Main Types of the Idea of the Atonement* (London: SPCK, 1953), p. 86.

24. Rudolf Bultmann, *Jesus Christ and Mythology* (New York: Charles Scribner's, 1958), p. 17.

25. J. Y. Lee, "Bultmann's Existentialist Interpretation and the Problem of Evil," *Journal of Religious Thought* 26 (Autumn-Winter 1969):73.

26. Dietrich Bonhoeffer, *Creation and Fall* (London: SCM, 1959), p. 53.

27. Huston Smith, *The Religions of Man* (New York: Harper and Row, 1958), pp. 188–89.

28. Mircea Eliade, *The Two and the One*, trans. J. M. Cohen (New York: Harper and Row, 1965), p. 96.

29. *Tao te ching*, chap. 27.

30. Ibid., chap. 57.

31. This kind of dualism has been widespread. There is, for example, the Russian myth that presupposes that neither God nor the Devil were created, but have coexisted from the beginning of the world. See Eliade, *The Two and the One*, p. 85. The Persian (Zoroastrian) myth of struggle between the good spirit (Ormazd) and the evil (Ahriman), which dates from the seventh century B.C., was the source of the dualistic worldview of the later Judeo-Christian tradition.

32. Garma C. C. Chang, *The Buddhist Teaching of Totality* (University Park: Penn State University Press, 1971), p. 131.

33. Carl Michalson, *The Hinge of History: An Existential Approach to the Christian Faith* (New York: Scribner's Sons, 1959), p. 153.

34. Paul Schilling, *God in an Age of Atheism* (Nashville: Abingdon Press, 1969), p. 215.

35. Nels F. S. Ferré, *The Universal Word: A Theology for a Universal Faith* (Philadelphia: Westminster, 1969), p. 80.

36. Ibid., p. 100.

37. Schubert Ogden, *The Reality of God and Other Essays* (New York: Harper and Row, 1966), p. 48.

CHAPTER IV

CHANGE AS THE SOURCE OF CREATIVITY: GOD AS CREATOR

That God is creator of the world is the most important affirmation of Judeo-Christian faith, its importance clearly attested by its position in the Bible, whose opening words define God as the creator: "In the beginning God created heaven and earth." That affirmation is the unquestioned core of Judeo-Christian faith and is prior to all its other affirmations. God as savior, ruler, and preserver presupposes God as creator. That is why the earliest Christian authors made God as creator the first person of the Trinity.

THE NEGLECTED CREATOR GOD

Yet the Christian church, in its emphasis on the savior God, has almost forgotten the primary importance of the creator God. Hinduism reveals the same shift in historical emphasis. India contains only a few temples of the creator God, Brahma, but numberless temples to the gods of preservation and destruction, Vishnu and Shiva. Brahma is almost forgotten by Hindus because they consider that his purpose has been accomplished. Shiva, the god of destruction, who later became also the god of renewal, has become the most important God of the Hindu trinity because his purpose has yet to be accomplished.

The history of Christian belief seems to follow the same pattern. Christians' primary devotion is not to the God of creation but to the God of renewal or salvation, because salvation has not yet been accomplished. As early as the fourth and fifth centuries questions of redemption or soteriology had become the most important element in christological and trinitarian controversies. Preoccupation with the concept of salvation had led Christians consciously or unconsciously to stress the importance of God as savior, who came to identify himself as Jesus Christ. Almost all the great Christian theologians—St. Augustine, Thomas Aquinas, Martin Luther, John Calvin, Karl Barth, Rudolf Bultmann, Paul Tillich, Dietrich Bonhoeffer, Wolfhart Pannenberg, among others—have concentrated on the person and works of Christ. Moreover, in the western church the doctrine of the Trinity does not indicate the functional priority of creator over redeemer. Father, Son, and Holy Spirit have been made coeval. Only in the eastern church is the priority of creator over redeemer recognized in the doctrine of the Trinity, where the Son follows the Father and the Holy Spirit follows the Son.

Western Christianity's undue neglect of creation and emphasis on salvation has made Christ the savior more important than God the creator, and this Christocentric theology has in turn had the unfortunate effect of making Christianity an exclusive religion. But Jesus said again and again that he came to fulfill the work of his Father, the creator. He never said that his Father's work had been only a prelude to his own. On the contrary, Jesus' redemptive work was but an extension of his Father's creative work. Thus creation is the a priori category of redemption. Theology's proper subject, then, is divine creativity rather than divine redemptivity, because the former includes the latter.

CREATOR-CENTERED THEOLOGY

The theology of change must be creator-centered rather than savior-centered or Christ-centered. Creator-centered theology is compatible with the contemporary worldview that the world is not something "done" or completed but is in process. According to the theory of relativity the world is not static but is in constant change and transformation. Nuclear physics provides evidence that everything, including subatomic particles, is in motion and in transition. In other words, the world is to be known in terms of the process of becoming rather than in terms of the state of being. Creation is a continuing process rather than a singular event, because God the creator is alive. Thus to stress God's role as creator is to see the ever evolving universe as his work. Since God's creativity is an ongoing process toward the fuller realization of the divine consciousness in us, God's redemptive activity is part of his creative activity. Christ's redemptive activity is part of God's creative activity in the world; therefore, in creator-centered theology Christ is the perfect symbol of divine creativity.

Creator-centered theology also opens Christianity to ecumenical contact with other world religions. Christianity became an exclusive religion by stressing the redemptive aspect of God, that is, by making Christ its primary object of faith. But by looking upon God primarily as creator, we establish a bond with other religions. For example, Christianity accepts the Judaic account of the creation as it is expressed in Genesis; it is Christianity's overwhelming emphasis on redemption (and consequent slighting of creation) that has so thoroughly divorced it from its Judaic origins. By understanding redemption to be part of creation, we not only clarify our own faith but recover our Old Testament heritage, the heritage of Judaism. Since God's creativity seems to be the common denominator uniting different religions, interpreting Christ's redemptive work as an extension of God's creative work creates a basis for ecumenical rapprochement with Judaism, Islam, and also with other world religions. The major eastern religions—Hinduism, Buddhism, Taoism, and Shintoism—assert that the constantly changing world reveals an ongoing process of divine creativity. Therefore, Christian emphasis on God's creative process in the world makes possible genuine ecumenical dialogue with other world religions.

GOD AS THE SOURCE OF CREATIVITY

Let us examine the traditional Judeo-Christian idea of God as the sole source of creativity. The account of creation as *creatio ex nihilo* ("creation out of nothing") is often said to be unique to Judeo-Christian tradition. The idea that God created the world *out of nothing* appears for the first time in the literature of later Judaism, but it is compatible with the biblical tradition. As Jacob says, "*Creatio ex nihilo* is found explicitly affirmed for the first time in Second Maccabees (7:28); 'Consider the heaven and the earth . . . and know that God has not made them from existing things, '*ouk ezonton epoiesen auta*; the reading presupposed by the Syriac version and the Vulgate was *ez ouk onton*, which accentuates still further the creation *ex nihilo*."[1] This doctrine implies unmistakably that the sole source of creativity is the creator; it denies the dualistic possibility that creation was formed by the creator out of some other independently existing source.[2]

The word "nothing," or *nihilo*, must be understood not as a "chaos or darkness" that existed independently of God, but as nonbeing, which is the root of creativeness. Nicholas Berdyaev says, "Creation means transition from non-being through a free act."[3] This transition from nonbeing, or "no-thing," to being, or "thing," is the essence of "*creatio ex nihilo*." Since the Judeo-Christian faith is so essentially monotheistic, nonbeing, the root of being, must be the creator. In other words, the creator is nonbeing or "no-thing" that becomes the source of all things. As Lao Tzu says, "All things in the world come from being. All being comes from non-being."[4] God as creator is more than a mere "maker" or ruler of his creations; he is their sole source and origin. If God simply made the world out of pre-existing stuff, then God would be merely the shaper and not the source of all things. But God created us out of "no-thing"—meaning out of himself. In this respect orthodox Christian theology's infinite qualitative distinction between God and humankind simply does not exist.

"No-thing," or nonbeing, as the creative source of all things is more clearly expressed in the Buddhist idea of nirvana, the ultimate reality. The literal meaning of nirvana is "to blow out" or "to extinguish." It is the absolute annihilation, that is, the absolute nonexistence, from which all the creative process evolves. Nirvana in this respect resembles the ultimate reality known to Christian mystics as godhead. Edward Conze remarks, "when we compare the attributes of the Godhead, as they are understood by the more mystical tradition of Christian thought, with those of Nirvana, we find almost no difference at all."[5]

Nirvana as godhead is the source of all existence. Thus Buddha said, "There is, O monks, an Unborn, neither become nor created nor formed. . . . Were there not there would be no deliverance from the born, the made, the compounded."[6] That is why nirvana, or the Mahayana concept of *śūnyatā*, is not nihilism or acosmism but the affirmation of the ultimate reality that is beyond created existence. Therefore it is closely related to change, which is the *t'ai chi*, or Great Ultimate.[7] "The Great Ultimate is fundamentally the Non-Ultimate."[8] This nonultimate as change generates *yin* and *yang* and produces all things. Therefore it is the nonultimate or nonbeing that becomes the source of creative existence for all things. God as creator (or ultimate reality) creates everything out of himself (or the nonultimate). Ultimate and nonultimate are identical; they are God.

Human beings create out of the created, but God creates out of nothing. There was no pre-existing "chaos" or "darkness" out of which God created—only God himself. Creatures can never create; they can only reshape the already created. God alone can create out of nothing, because that nothing is himself. God's giving of himself in the process of creativity is the meaning of *agape* ("love"). If there were no self-giving in the process of creation, God would not be the God of love, the God of self-giving love. *Agape* is more than God's action. It is God's own nature: "God is love" (1 John 4:8,11). Bonhoeffer makes this point clearly: "Love is not what He *does* and what He *suffers*, but it is what *He* does and what *He* suffers. Love is always He Himself. Love is always God Himself."[9] The doctrine of "creation out of nothing" denies the dualistic worldview and at the same time affirms God's self-giving in the process of creation. If God in the process of creation does not act upon anything extraneous to himself but rather gives himself, then the creature is a manifestation of the creator.

In other words, there is an essential continuum between the creator and the creature. But in the history of Christian thought this essential continuum has been mostly ignored or con-

tradicted. Augustine's doctrine of original sin, strongly reinforced by Calvinism, asserts or implies an infinite qualitative
distinction between the divinity and humanity that has been
maintained by Kierkegaard and by Karl Barth and his followers.
The doctrine of original sin forced theologians to question the
analogy of being between God and humanity.[10] But humanity's
Fall did not destroy the *essential* continuum between God and
us—that is inherent in our creation out of God and cannot be
destroyed by our sin. It destroyed only the *existential* continuum.
The essential relationship is the ontic continuity between creator
and creature.

What is meant by ontic continuity, or essential relationship,
between creator and creature? First of all, it means that God and
the world are inseparable. Where there is creature, there must be
creator. The creature is brought into being out of and by the
action of the creator. Therefore the creator is more than a mere
participant in the affairs of the world. The creature may not
recognize the creator's presence because of existential distortion,
which obstructs God's essential presence, but there is no way
that the creature can be cut off from the creator, because God's
essential presence is always primordial in the existence of the
creature. Since the creature's acts are always contingent upon the
act of the creator, nothing the creature may do can destroy the
relationship established by the creator. But though the creator is a
part of us, his primacy makes him ineradicably different from us.
In Hartshorne's words: "What does distinguish God is that the
preceding phase was itself created by God so that he, unlike us, is
never confronted by a world whose coming to be antedates his
own entire existence. There is no presupposed 'stuff' alien to
God's creative work; but rather everything that influences God
has already been influenced by him, whereas we are influenced
by events of the past with which we had nothing to do."[11]

What distinguishes God from humankind are his functional
primacy and eminency. Being the creator of heaven and earth
means that God "is the basis of all things and all that exists only
exists by his will."[12] He is not only a part of creativity but also the
source of it. To be the source of creativity is more than creativity
itself; it is transcendence. This transcendental nature of God

makes him the creator. Perhaps that is why Whitehead seems to avoid the term "creator" for God,[13] preferring to speak of God and the world as counterparts.[14] God as the creator must transcend the process of creativity that is ofen considered the ultimate. Neveille might be right in saying that the process God "is in no way the ground or source of the being of finite things."[15] God as creator transcends the categories of process and creativity, because he is the source of them while participating in them. The essential continuum between creator and creature does not preclude divine transcendence. Traditional descriptions of God as inexhaustible or hidden may be metaphors for the creator's divine transcendence. God is not limited to his manifestation in the world of becoming. His quality of infinitude exceeds all the perfections of finitude. Divinity is more than creativity.

In distinguishing between God as the creator and the process of creativity, it will be helpful to examine the concept of change expressed in the *I ching,* which deals most profoundly with the metaphysics of cosmology. According to the *I ching* the world is an ever-changing flux and process of creation because of change, which is the source as well as part of that changing world. Change is not only primary to and pre-eminent over all manifested changes; it also transcends them. Its transcendence lies in its infinite and inexhaustible concentration of the power of change. As the source of the creative power of becoming, change transcends the world while being a part of it. As the Great Commentary to the *I ching* says, "The begetter of all begetting is called the Change."[16] Change is more than creativity; it is the source of all that is and that will be. Existence presupposes creativity, and creativity presupposes change. Since creativity is inherent in the process of change, change is prior to creativity. Therefore change is identical with God the creator, who is not only the creative process but also its source.

CREATOR AND CREATURE

In the second place, the ontic continuity, or essential relationship between creator and creature, means that there is an inner relationship in the form of a covenant between them. Karl Barth calls this covenant the internal basis of the creation and the creation the external basis of the covenant.[17] According to Barth the Ten Commandments—the historical manifestation of the essential relationship between creator and creature—could have been given at Sinai only because the covenant had existed within the godhead before the process of creation. In other words, Barth asserts the priority of covenant over creation, because the former embodies the internal relationship between creator and creature and the latter the external relationship. God's internal, *covenantal* relationship with the world is prior to his external, *creating* relationship. Both together constitute the ontic continuum between creator and creature, but the covenant pre-exists and makes possible the creativity. The inner, covenantal relationship is distinguished from the external, creative relationship by its directness. The internal relationship is the *im-mediated* relationship, while the external relationship is the mediated relationship. This *im-mediated* relationship is clearly expressed in Barth's idea of covenant within the godhead, especially between the Father and the Son. The Son represents humankind or the world, the Father the creator. The covenantal relationship between Father and Son in eternity is repeated in history between creator and creature. The profundity of this idea consists in locating the inner relationship within God, who is one God yet is known as Father, Son, and Holy Spirit. What happens between Father and Son in the oneness of divine nature can be understood as the archetype of what happens between Subject and subject in the process of creativity.

The external relationship, on the other hand, is a subject-object relationship. The former is often called the "I-Thou" relationship, the latter the "I-It" relationship. These categories are mutually interdependent, just as the covenant and creation are mutually inclusive. One cannot exist without the other. Even though the "I-Thou" relationship is prior, it is inseparable from the "I-It" relationship, because of the essential continuity between the creator and the creature, which is the objectifying process in creation. In this kind of mutually inclusive relationship the covenant, which embodies the "I-Thou" relationship, cannot be static. It is as dynamic and changing as creation is in the process of change. The covenant is more than a mere contract; it is the dynamic and living personal relationship made possible by the essential continuum between creator and creature. Just as the covenant makes creation possible, the internal relationship makes the external relationship possible. As Moltmann says, "The covenant will have to be understood as a history-making event which opens up specific possibilities of history."[18]

In other words, the process of creativity is possible because of the *im-mediated* relationship between creator and creature that is the inner essence of creativity. In terms of the essential process of creativity this *im-mediated* relationship means that the creator is change, the source of all creative process in the world. The inner change that constitutes divine nature is essentially related to the world's manifest, external changing. That is why the *i*, or change, is often called the begetter of all begetting and the source of all creativity.[19] Change must then be the "moving mover" rather than the "unmoved mover," and "changing changer" rather than the "changeless one." The "moving mover" (or "changing changer") is the symbol of the inner change that is manifested in the creative process of the external world. Essential continuity lies in change, which is both internal and external. If we regard the covenant as the internal relationship of change in eternity, creation is the external relationship of the changing process. Creation as change itself constitutes the covenant in process, and the covenant in process makes possible the creation in process. Thus the world is in process of becoming.

The idea of the covenant helps us further to define the relationship between creator and creature. In both their *im-mediated* and mediated relationships the creator is more than a mere contrastable partner of the creature, because the creator is always the subject of the creature. The creature must always be the object of the creator, because the creature has no existence without the creator. The creature can never become the creator's subject, nor the creator the creature's object, because the creator is always the Subject of his creation. Let us return to Barth's idea of the covenant: In the invisible, eternal covenant between Father and Son the Son represents the creature and the Father the creator. By virtue of these representations the Father acts as subject and the

Son as object. Since the Son who symbolizes the creature is also divine, creator and creature are essentially one and inseparable.

Ontic continuity between creator and creature thus entails essential unity between divine subject and divine object, which in turn entails the essential unity between creator as the creature's subject and creature as the creator's object. The creator is the eternal Subject of his creature as well as the Subject of his own Son. God, by saying to Moses from the burning bush, "I am what I am," or "I become what I become" (Exod. 3:1–15), affirms that he is our eternal Subject and never our object. At the same time, he also affirms his is-ness, which is beyond our objectification. He is object of himself without becoming object of his creature. God as subject is often called the basis of existence —without him neither people nor any part of creation could be. He is the true self of all things, personal or impersonal.

This concept of God as the true self in all things is explicitly called, in the Upanishads, Ātman: "Ātman, smaller than the small, greater than the great, is hidden in the hearts of all living creatures."[20] Ātman is identical with Brahman, the cosmic self. The former is the microcosm of the latter. Thus the famous formula *"tat tvam asi"* ("that art thou") expresses the essential relationship between the individual self and the cosmic self, the ultimate reality. The identity between the individual self, the Ātman, and the cosmic self, the Brahman, provides the ontic continuity between creator and creature. In this self or Subject, microcosmic and macrocosmic worlds find their essential unity.

The world and God are united but not identical, because God is the eternal subject of the world and the world is the objectification of God. As Pittenger says, "The world is *in* God, and God is *in* the world, he penetrates it and works through it and employs it for this purpose, but he is himself *not* the world nor anything in the world, not even human nature at its best."[21] The creator's transcendence consists in his subjectivity to his creatures. He is the primordial change of all the changing world because of his subjectivity. Change as the subject of all changes controls everything that changes. Change is *in* everything that changes, but everything that changes is not change.[22] Everything that changes is a phenomenon of change, but the change itself is changeless because it is Subject of the changing phenomena. Finally, ontic continuity between creator and creature means that humanity is essentially identical to all other created phenomena. Humanity is essentially one with trees, grasses, stones, animals, and all other living and nonliving creatures in the world—not in existential manifestation but in essential nature. The *imago Dei* (the "likeness of God") does not make humanity unique among creatures. As we have pointed out in the previous chapter, contemporary theologians repudiate the idea that humanity is essentially made in God's image to set us above or in any way apart from other creatures. Bonhoeffer says, "The likeness, the analogy of man to God, is not *analogia entis* but *analogia relationis.* This means that even the relation between Man and God is not a part of man; it is not a capacity, a possibility, or a structure of his being but a given, set relationship: *justitia passiva.* . . . *Analogia relationis* is, therefore, the relation given by God himself and is analogy only in His relation given by God."[23]

If the image of God is the analogy of relation—the essential relationship in which God extends himself to humanity—then all other creatures are also the likeness of God, because God extends himself to them as he extends himself to us.[24] Therefore, creation in the image of God or the likeness of God does not preclude ontic continuity between humanity and other creatures. Humanity is certainly created out of dust. The Bible says, "God formed man of dust from the ground" (Gen. 2:7). Thus humanity has its origin with all other things. "Man's origin is in a piece of earth. His bond with the earth belongs to his essential being. The 'earth is his mother'; he comes out of her womb."[25] So says Bonhoeffer, echoing Chang Tsai, one of the pioneers of Neo-Confucian philosophy, nine centuries before: "Heaven is my father and earth is my mother, and even such a small creature as I finds an intimate place in their midst. Therefore that which extends throughout the universe I regard as my body and that which directs the universe I consider as my nature. All people are my brothers and sisters, and all things are my companions."[26]

In China heaven, earth, and humanity form a trinity, which is clearly depicted in the trigrams of the *I ching.* As explained in the previous chapter, heaven represents the creator, earth the creation, and humanity the mediator of heaven and earth. The trigrams affirm the ontic continuity among creator, creation, and humanity, and Chang Tsai's *Hsi-ming* gives this continuity clear and poignant expression. Bonhoeffer has brought eastern wisdom to bear on the traditional theistic interpretation of humanity. If humanity's essential being comes from the earth, then we and all other creatures share the same origin or source, which is the creator himself. "The earth is [our] mother," as heaven is our father, and the differences between these are existential rather than essential, or functional rather than ontic.

ORDERS OF CREATIVE PROCESS

The ontic unity of all things consists of *yin* and *yang*, which represent earth and heaven. Everything is the product of both *yin* and *yang*, which are generative forms of change. This idea is clearly expressed in the biblical account of the creation: "In the beginning God created the heavens and the earth" (Gen. 1:1). The corresponding statement in the Great Commentary to the Book of Changes reads: "The Supreme Ultimate is in the *I* or the change. It produces the two forms."[27] These two forms are *yang* and *yin*, or heaven and earth. Heaven, represented by the first hexagram, *ch'ien*, consists entirely of *yang* lines, while earth, represented by the second hexagram, *k'un*, consists entirely of *yin* lines. *Ch'ien* is the pure form of *yang* (or positive energy), and *k'un* is the pure form of *yin* (or negative energy). Thus heaven and earth, or *ch'ien* and *k'un*, are the prototypes of *yang* and *yin* elements in all things. "In the beginning God created the heavens and the earth" seems to correspond to the idea that in the beginning the change (or the *i*) generated the *ch'ien* (the first hexagram) and the *k'un* (the second hexagram). Since everything in the world is the product of these two prototypes of energy, this statement summarizes the creation. Just as heaven and earth contain everything, the hexagrams *ch'ien* and *k'un* represent everything and produce by interaction all the possible microcosmic situations that are symbolized by the sixty-four germinal situations (hexagrams) in the *I ching*.

Reading further in the biblical creation story we find the image of darkness distinguished from light and water from dry land. In the *I ching* darkness and water are *yin,* light and *terra firma* are *yang.* The biblical creation story depicts the process of creative evolvement in which *yin* and *yang* became the primary categories of all other creative moments.[28] *Yin* and *yang* are microcosms of earth and heaven; they also correspond to female and male in species, below and above in space, evil and good in human deeds, and counterpoles of all other things in creation. Their interplay creates and moves all things. Thus change is not only the source of these two forces but also operates through them. The creator as change is the source of these two primary forces through which he works or changes the world in the process of becoming. This kind of creative process seems apparent from our study of the physical world. Everything in the atomic structure can be reduced to two different electronic charges. The nucleon of atoms consists of protons and neutrons, which are now considered two different electronic states of the same element.[29] That is, the proton is a charged neutron and the neutron is an uncharged proton.[30] The electrons that move around the nuclei are also born in pairs.[31] Thus contemporary science has found that interacting negative and positive forces, *yin* and *yang,* make the process of creation possible.

The Bible seems to suggest that these forces of creativity are the activity of the creator and come from him, but explains them no further. And as Henry Margenau, Yale University physicist, says, "Physics is no longer adequate to guide man in his quest into matter. We know the composition of the atom, but now we need metaphysics to help us to understand why the subatomic particles act as they do. Why do two electrons go into orbit around a nucleus of protons and neutrons and form helium? And why two?"[32]

In the *I ching,* however, are some clues to the creative process of these two forces. In the *I ching* the germinal situations, which might be compared with subatomic structures, are symbolized by hexagrams. These germinal situations are in constant flux, as electronic charges in atomic structures are in constant flow. They are the combinations of positive and negative, or *yang* and *yin* lines. Their flux is represented by the lines of hexagrams changing from *yin* to *yang* and from *yang* to *yin*, which may be compared to the negative changing to positive and the positive changing to negative. These changes create fields similar to the magnetic fields enclosing atomic structures.

According to the metaphysics of the *I ching* the microcosmic event of change is simple and easy: Cosmic change occurs through union and separation. The undivided line (——), which represents *yang* force, becomes the divided line (— —), the *yin* force, through separation. The divided line (— —) resumes its undivided form (——) through union. Thus "the union and separation of *yin* and *yang* are similar to the opening and closing gates of heaven and earth. Just as everything in the universe proceeds from heaven and earth toward interaction, all things are procreation of the union and separation of *yin* and *yang* forces."[33] The *I ching*, though not a scientific text, attempts to describe the fundamental principle of the creative process in the world as the uniting and separating of opposites by the power of change. Therefore change as the creator works in all things, from micro- to macrocosmic structures. It works in the world as the changing force that "forms the plants and gives the animals their food" (Ps. 145:15; 147:8; Job 38:39) and "gives light each day" (Amos 5:8), so that the world is in constant process of becoming.

CHANGE AS THE CREATOR

Let us summarize our conclusions about change as the creator. Traditional theology's failure has lain in stressing God's redemptive aspect at the expense of his creative aspect. Because early Christians considered human redemption to be of central importance, traditional theology has concentrated on the redeemer rather than the creator. But the Bible accords greater eminence to the creator than to his Son the redeemer. Redemption originates, according to the Bible, in and by action of the creator, and is therefore part of and subsidiary to creation. Therefore the creator, who is the Father, should be, and is, the main object of theological inquiry in the theology of change.

That God is creator is the primary and central affirmation of Judeo-Christian tradition. The Hebraic beliefs in absolute monotheism and a world in process are basic to our study of God's creative work. Dualistic and static worldviews are as incompatible with the central teachings of Old and New Testament as they are with the contemporary worldview. If the classical doctrine of creation, *creatio ex nihilo*, is analyzed in monotheistic and dynamic terms, *nothing*, or *nonbeing* can be understood, not only as the negation of everything that exists, but also as the affirmation of all that can exist *in potentia*. This *nonbeing* from which the world is created is expressed in the Buddhist concept of nirvana, which is both the complete absence of all beings and the source of all possible beings. According to the inclusive way of thinking, which is our method, *being* presupposes *nonbeing*; *nonbeing* is not only the absence of being but also the source of *being*.

Since the Judeo-Christian faith absolutely denies a dualistic worldview, the *nonbeing* that is the source of *being* can only be the creator. In this respect, *nonbeing* is analogous to nirvana, or change, which is the ultimate reality. The world that is created out of *nothing* is created out of the creator himself. The idea that God is love proceeds from the idea that God is the source of creation. Therefore, there must be an ontic, or essential, continuum between creator and creatures. Essentially, creator and creatures are inseparably one; they differ only in existential manifestations. The Judeo-Christian creator is comparable to the Hindu Ātman, the true self of all things. He is the absolute Subject and center of creative process.

Careful examination of the Old Testament's creation story reveals a dynamic worldview, expressed in terms of creative evolvement from heaven and earth, which is compatible with the idea of changing process in the *I ching*. Traditional theology blinded us to the essential continuum between creator and creature by positing a mechanistic rather than an organic creation. In the mechanistic worldview God as the creator is a mere agent of creation, like an artisan who creates a static product out of preexisting materials. But the world as the Hebrews understood it and as we understand it now is a constantly evolving and changing organism that was created by God out of God. Just as a child is essentially one with, though existentially separate from, its progenitors, from the organic point of view God as creator is source as well as agent of his creatures.

Because the organic worldview is widespread in the East, so also is the idea of organic process of creation. In the Upanishads the creator is often symbolized by the spider, which sends forth and draws in its thread in the process of creation.[34] Moreover the creative process evolves out of *Purusha,* the cosmic person, from whom are born *"prāna,* mind, all the sense-organs, *ákása,* air, fire, water, and earth, which supports all."[35] Creation is similar to the organic process of procreation, which begins with the one, the Absolute, which is Brahman, and then proceeds with multiplication and growth. According to the Upanishads the creative process begins in thought rather than word: "It [Brahman] thought: 'May I be many; may I grow forth.' It created fire."[36] Lao Tzu describes the creative process similarly: "Tao produced the one. The one produced the two. The two produced the three. And the three produced the ten thousand things."[37]

Creation is a process of evolvement from one to many, that is, a process of differentiation from the undifferentiated continuum. In the Old Testament, too, the creative process is a process of multiplication through differentiation—of light from darkness, heaven from earth, dry land from water, male from female, and so on. The *I ching* likewise presents the process of creation as one of multiplication through differentiation. The eleventh-century Neo-Confucian philosopher Shao Yung, influenced by the *I ching* and by Lao Tzu, not only posited but charted such a cosmology.[38] According to his charts, the Great Ultimate (太 極) differentiated into two: *Yin* (陰) and *yang* (陽). These differentiate into new *yin* and old *yin,* new *yang* and old *yang.* This process of differentiation results in the formation of sixty-four hexagrams, which are presented as the archetypes of every possible form of manifestation. In each of these manifestations either *yin* or *yang* is dominant, but in no case does one wholly supplant the other. "The process recalls the phenomena seen in the morphogenesis of many animals (e.g., echinoderms, fishes, amphibia), for which it has been necessary to develop the conception of morphogenetic fields."[39] In other words, the creative process of evolvement by means of differentiation retains the essential continuum in all

Diagram of Cosmic Evolution in Terms of the Sixty-four Hexagrams

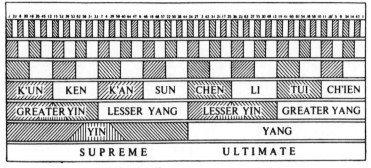

Numbers at top are those of Sixty-four **Hexagrams**
Names in middle are those of Eight **Trigrams**

things. Since the Judeo-Christian worldview is dynamic as well as organic, we can interpret the symbolic description of the creative process in Genesis in terms of morphogenesis, the structural differentiation of organisms. In that kind of creative process creatures are distinguished from one another, but all retain the nature of the creator. Therefore all creatures are united with each other and with the creator.

The change that generates change in all things is the creator, the Subject of all creation and the power that unites and separates *yin* and *yang* in all things. This power to separate and unite the primordial forces is the Word, which the creator pronounced in the process of creation. The Word accompanied the creation: "God said, 'Let there be light'; and there was light" (Gen. 1:3). In the New Testament (John 1:14) this Word is known as the Christ. Thus Christ is creativity, which seems to be Paul's meaning: "He [Christ] is the image of the invisible God, the first-born of all creation; for in him all things were created, in heaven and on earth, visible and invisible, whether thrones or dominions or principalities or authorities—all things were created through him and for him. He is before all things, and in him all things hold together" (Col. 1:15–17). In essence Paul is describing Christ as the power of the primordial forces of *yin* and *yang*, the source for all time of all creative processes.

Notes

1. Edmond Jacob, *Theology of the Old Testament,* trans. Arthur W. Heathcote and Philip J. Allcock (New York: Harper & Brothers, 1958), p. 143, note 1.

2. Cf. Emil Brunner, *The Christian Doctrine of Creation and Redemption: Dogmatics,* trans. Olive Wyon (Philadelphia: The Westminster Press, 1952), 2:10.

3. Nicolas Berdyaev, *The Destiny of Man* (New York: Harper & Brothers, 1960), p. 33.

4. *Tao te ching,* 40 (Wing-tsit Chan's translation).

5. Edward Conze, *Buddhism: Its Essence and Development* (New York: Philosophical Library, 1951), p. 39.

6. *Iti-vuttaka,* 43; *Udana,* VIII, 3.

7. *Ta chuan,* VI, 5.

8. Chou Tun-i, *T'ai-chi-t'u* (An Explanation of the Diagram of the Great Ultimate); cf. Wade Baskin, ed., *Classics in Chinese Philosophy* (New York: Philosophical Library, 1972), p. 454.

9. Dietrich Bonhoeffer, *Ethics* (New York: The Macmillan Company, 1955), p. 174.

10. Aquinas's doctrine of analogy of being was not only questioned but accused of being un-Christian. See J. Y. Lee, "Karl Barth's Use of Analogy in His Church Dogmatics," *Scottish Journal of Theology* 22, no. 2 (June 1969):133ff.

11. Charles Hartshorne, *The Divine Relativity: A Social Conception of God* (New Haven: Yale University Press, 1948, 1964), p. 30.

12. Jacob, *Theology of the Old Testament,* p. 37.

13. Alfred N. Whitehead, *Process and Reality* (New York: Macmillan, 1929), pp. 344, 519–20, 526.

14. Ibid., pp. 30, 47, 134, 344, 374.

15. Robert Neveille, *God the Creator* (Chicago: University of Chicago Press, 1968), p. 78.

16. *Ta chuan,* sec. I, ch. 5.

17. In the first part of his third volume of *Church Dogmatics.* Its English translation has been published by T. and T. Clark, Edinburgh, 1958.

18. Jürgen Moltmann, *Theology of Hope: On the Ground and the Implica-*

tions of a Christian Eschatology (New York and Evanston: Harper and Row, 1967), p. 121.

19. The *i*, or the change, produces two modes, *yin* and *yang*, which are the source of all changes and transformations. See *Ta chuan*, sec. I, ch. 2.

20. *Katha Upanishad*, I, ii, 20.

21. Norman Pittenger, *God in Process* (London: SCM Press, 1967), p. 27.

22. J. Y. Lee, *Cosmic Religion* (New York: Philosophical Library, 1973), p. 15.

23. Dietrich Bonhoeffer, *Creation and Fall* (London: SCM Press, 1959), p. 37.

24. The analogy of relation, however, drastically undercuts possible continuity between God and creature. As Emil Brunner points out, the *analogia relationis* cannot replace the *analogia entis* because the former presupposes the latter (see Brunner, *Christian Doctrine of Creation and Redemption*, p. 24). Barth later admitted the necessity of the analogy of being to his theological task (see Karl Barth, *The Humanity of God*, Richmond: John Knox, 1960, p. 44).

25. Bonhoeffer, *Creation and Fall*, p. 44.

26. This translation of the *Hsi-ming* (Western Inscription) is found in *Sources of Chinese Tradition*, comp. Wm. Theodore de Bary, Wing-tsit Chang, and Burton Watson, text ed. in 2 vols. (New York: Columbia University Press, 1964), 1:469.

27. *Ta chuan*, sec. I, ch. 11. Author's translation.

28. J. Y. Lee, *The I: A Christian Concept of Man* (New York: Philosophical Library, 1971), p. 28.

29. G. Gamow, *Mr. Thompkings in Paperback* (Cambridge: University Press, 1967), p. 136.

30. Kenneth Ford, *The World of Elementary Particles* (London: Blaisdell, 1963), p. 168.

31. Gamow, *Mr. Thompkings*, p. 125.

32. Quoted in Eric Butterworth, *Unity of All Life* (New York: Harper and Row, 1969), p. 22.

33. J. Y. Lee, *The Principle of Changes: Understanding the I Ching* (New Hyde Park, New York: University Books, 1971), p. 73.

34. *Mundaka Upanishad*, I, i, 7.

35. Ibid., II, i, 3.

36. *Chhāndogya Upanishad*, VI, ii, 3.

37. *Tao te ching*, 42.

38. See also the chart on p. 14 of this book.

39. Joseph Needham, *Science and Civilization in China* (Cambridge: Cambridge University Press, 1969), 2:276.

CHAPTER V

THE PERFECT REALIZATION
OF CHANGE: JESUS CHRIST

Christology has been the subject of theological controversy since the Christian church came into being. The first ecumenical council was called at Nicea in 325 to define the nature of Christ, which necessitates defining the nature of the Trinity. The fundamental issue at Nicea was salvation. Athanasius maintained Christ's divine essence against the Arian heresy as a matter of life and death for the church, because Christ's nature pertains directly to human salvation. The council at Chalcedon in 451 attempted to end the controversy by a formulation designed to answer the problem of salvation. Tillich perceived correctly that "the early Church was well aware that Christology is an existentially necessary, though not a theoretically interesting, work of the Church. Its ultimate criterion, therefore, is existential itself. It is 'soteriological,' i.e., determined by the question of salvation. The greater the things we say about the Christ, the greater the salvation we can expect from him."[1]

In other words, the christological question was directly related to the soteriological need of the church and for that reason acquired enormous theological importance. That is why Christian theology has paid more attention to Christ and his work than to God as creator and has commonly regarded the event of salvation as distinct from, and more important than, the event of creation. In other words, the continuity between God's creative work and his saving work has in the past been largely ignored, the saving work being attributed exclusively to the Christ and the creative work to the Father. Almost all past theology disjoins the doctrine of salvation from that of creation, giving the impression that the creation was a discrete event occurring prior to salvation.

The disjunction between salvation and creation, or between the Christ and his Father, resulted primarily from the Euclidian worldview, according to which discrete events take place in a linear time sequence. According to this worldview creation was accomplished in a given period of time and salvation came afterward. This tendency to separate creation from redemption was reinforced by the exclusive, or "either-or," way of thinking, according to which God's creative work must *either* precede his redemptive work *or* follow it. Since, according to this view, creation and redemption must be separate events, then it is right to consider Christ the redeemer separate from God the creator. In reality, however, God the savior and God the creator are one and inseparable. Although they are one, they are not identical; there is a functional difference between them. God as creator is prior to God as savior.

There is much evidence to support the idea that God's creativity is prior to his saving process in the world. If we attribute saving efficacy to the Christ and the creative process to the creator, we see clearly the functional primacy of the latter. Salvation is presupposed in creation, but creation is absolutely necessary to salvation because salvation means a return to the original creation.[2] Moreover Jesus Christ said again and again that he came to the world to fulfill the will of his Father, the creator. Christ's work, the work of salvation, was the extension of his Father's work, the work of creation. If Christ came to do his Father's work, then what Christ did, the work of salvation, was the creator's work. Therefore salvation is contingent on creation, not the other way around. Christ's work as savior must be understood as the extension of the creator's work, that is, as God's continuing work of creation in the world. If Christ as savior did his Father's work out of filial piety, we must not attribute that work to Christ alone, since Christ did it for his Father. If Christ had done the work of salvation independently of his Father, then the work of salvation might be Christ's alone. But the testimony of New Testament witnesses makes it almost unthinkable to separate the work of Christ from that of his Father. The role of savior is a subsidiary part of the role of creator.

PROBLEMS OF CHRISTOLOGY

The trinitarian doctrine propounded by the early church is therefore mistaken: Christ is not coequal with his Father who "sent" him to do his work. Emil Brunner, who takes the trinitarian doctrine seriously, believes that the early church, failing to understand the specific and necessary hierarchy, or precedence, of the Father, the Son, and the Holy Spirit, placed them side by side. Thus he says, "The theology of the Early Church, as we shall see, did not, it is true, alter this order, but since it had very little idea that this order 'mattered,' its teaching suggests three 'persons,' side by side; this had a disastrous effect upon the doctrine of God."[3] Nowhere in Scripture is the Son identified with the Father. Christ said, "I and the Father are one" (John 10:30), or "He who has seen me has seen the Father" (John 14:9), but he did *not* say, "I am the Father and the Father is I." The exigencies of salvation doctrine led the early church to make Christ coequal with the creator.

But God as the creator is the source of creativity and the source of all that is and will be, while Christ is only what is manifested of God. To identify the creator with the revealer, the Christ, is to deny the inexhaustible nature of the divine creativity. God as creator is more than what is manifested, and his mystery is not and will not be exhausted. He is more than the One revealed in Christ. God as creator is active where Christ is not. "Thus there are works of God which as such are precisely not works of the Son. This non-identity of God and the Son is based upon the fact that God alone is Creator, but that the Son is called simply and solely the mediator of the Creation."[4] In other words, Christ is subordinate to the creator, and his work as savior and redeemer is one part of the work of God as creator. Salvation is an element toward the consummation of creation. Everything that Jesus Christ has done or has been must be understood as an element of divine creativity. By such an approach we can correct the doctrinal errors brought about by undue emphasis on salvation alone.

CHRIST AS THE WORD

Christ as the foundation of the creative process is clearly expressed in the story of creation, where Christ is identical with the
Word coming from the mouth of the Creator. The creation story
may be the best place to begin the study of Christology, because
"the Word" is more expressive of Christ than any other name.
The Word was the basis of creative process: It had the power of
creativity. The story of creation in Genesis—not factual but
metaphorical—reveals profound truth. At each stage of the creative process God *speaks*, saying, "Let there be . . . " God's word,
in Genesis, is the power of generation; it is not a static, descriptive attribute of God. In Israel as in all the ancient Orient, in
contrast to classical Greece, God's word of utterance signified
dynamic force, the power of change and transformation.[5] As
Boman says, "In Israel also the divine word had an express
dynamic character and possessed a tremendous power."[6]
Jeremiah compares the power of the Word with "a fire, a hammer
that shatters the rocks" (Jer. 23:29). And Isaiah likens the power
of God's Word directly to the power of generation: "For as the
rain and the snow come down from heaven and return not thither
but water the earth, making it bring forth and sprout, giving seed
to the sower and bread to the eater, so shall my word be that goes
forth from my mouth; it shall not return to me empty, but it shall
accomplish that which I purpose, and prosper in the thing for
which I sent it" (Isa. 55:10–11).

Thus, to the Hebraic mind, Christ as the Word of God was not a
form or structure but the dynamic force that changes and produces new life and new possibilities. The Word, which in Greek
thought is analogous to Reason, is in the Hebrew mind almost
identical with the Deed of God.[7] Moreover, in the Fourth Gospel
the Greek word *logos*, while retaining its classical Greek connotation, has acquired the meaning of the Hebrew word, *dabhar*. In
other words, at the beginning of the Fourth Gospel "the Word"
means primarily the power of creativity rather than a form of
structure.

There is a close relationship between the first five verses of the

Fourth Gospel and the first five verses of Genesis. Both are cosmogonies: Both treat the story of creation, but from different perspectives.[8] Genesis narrates the creation in detail in order to emphasize that God is the creator. The Fourth Gospel summarizes the process of creation for the purpose of emphasizing that Christ is the Word. But the Fourth Gospel also explicitly states that the Word is the basis of God's creativity: "All things were made through him, and without him was not anything made that was made" (John 1:3). Certainly those words affirm that the Word is the creative power of God, and the next verse reaffirms it: "In him was life, and the life was the light of man" (John 1:4). "In him was life" can also be translated as "In the Word was life."[9] Of course, life and light are the most common metaphors of creative power to be found in nature. In the Old Testament they are considered the essential forces of creation and preservation: God gives life (Ezek. 37:1–14; Dan. 12:2), which is the source of light (Ps. 119:130). Today the formula is reversed: Life is sustained by light, which is the basis of energy. In either formulation Christ as the Word is to be understood as the energy that is the basis of creation and re-creation.

The Word that becomes the power of creative process is also the wisdom of God. In Proverbs 8:22–31 wisdom is personified and becomes God's instrument and architect in creation, bringing salvation to humankind. This idea undergoes further elaboration, and wisdom and Torah become one in the creative process. "It becomes a commonplace of rabbinic Judaism that Wisdom and Torah were one and the same, and therefore Torah was the pre-existent instrument of creation, without which nothing was made that was made; indeed, all that was made was created for the sake of the Torah."[10] Christ is "the image of the invisible God, the firstborn of all creation; for in him were all things created. . . . All things have been created through him and unto him" (Col. 1:15–17). Here Christ, "the image of the invisible God," is identified with the rabbinic definition of wisdom: Each is the focal point of creative process.[11] Thus wisdom (*sophia*), like the word (*dabhar*), signifies the creative activity of God. The creator, the source of creation, is the background of wisdom, and wisdom, or the Word, is the foreground of the creator. They are mutually interdependent in the process of creation and redemption. A similar idea occurs in the Mahayana Buddhist tradition, especially in *Prajñāpāramitā-Sutra,* in which wisdom, or *prajñā,* is united with *śūnyatā,* or nonbeing, as the source of creation. *Prajñā,* which is often translated as "transcendental wisdom" or "divine wisdom," is a counterpart of *śūnyatā,* or "emptiness." Suzuki says, "It is the *Prajñā* that sees into all implications of Emptiness [non-being]."[12] Like *prajñā,* Christ as wisdom represents the foreground of divine creativity, that is the light and life of the world.

CHRIST AS THE LIGHT

If we believe not only that Christ as Word or wisdom is "the first-born of all creation" but that "all things are created through him," he must be the basis for every creative process, including light and darkness, life and death. In him nothing is separated, whether good or evil. We notice, however, especially in the Fourth Gospel and in apocalyptic writings, that Christ as the symbol of light and life is in conflict with darkness and death. Even though nothing, including darkness and death, can be separated from God's love that is in Christ, these writings apparently exclude darkness and death from the realm of his redemptive love. But as we have seen, absolute monotheism renders this antithesis incidental and superficial. The conflict between light and darkness or between life and death, like all other conflicts, is not ultimate. It is not essential but existential. To define these conflicts as essential presupposes an erroneous dualism.

Christ as the Word or the core of creative process is the solution to the existential problem, the problem of estrangement or sin. Christ as the Word is God in existence, as differentiated from God in essence. Since Christ is God in existence, that is, God in manifestation, he is conditionally limited. Brunner says, "God [God as creator, or in essence] is present where Jesus Christ is not present with His Light and Life, in the darkness, as the God of wrath. Thus there are works of God which as such are precisely not works of the Son."[13] Brunner is partly right, but we may question his saying that Christ is not present in the darkness. Christ as light cannot be excluded from the darkness, because light cannot exist without darkness nor darkness without light. To exclude Christ from the darkness is in fact to exclude him from light also. Because Christ subjected himself to the condition of existence, the darkness must also be in his light. Conversely, Christ as light enters into our darkness.

The relationship between Christ as light and life and the world as darkness and death can be illustrated by the *Tai chi t'u,* the diagram of the Great Ultimate in the *I ching.*[14] The diagram consists of interlocked but differentiated *yin* (darkness) and *yang* (light). It is important to notice, however, that the *yin* portion of the diagram contains a *yang,* or light, dot, and the *yang* portion contains a *yin* dot. Christ as light, or *yang,* is not entirely exclusive of *yin,* or darkness, and the world as *yin,* or darkness, is not entirely exclusive of *yang* or light. The expansion of light (*yang*) in darkness (*yin*) is a metaphor of the process of redemption or the growth of Christ-consciousness in us. Redemption, which is Christ, grows within us just as we grow within Christ's redemptive work, which is part of his creative work. Tillich's definition of Christ as the solution to the problem of existential estrangement, or sin, is valid and useful.

CHRIST AS THE SAVIOR

Redemption, or salvation, presupposes the existential estrangement called sin. However we symbolize the concept of sin, we must remember that it is one of the possible relationships between creator and creature, or between the change and that which changes. The idea of existential estrangement resembles the Buddhist idea of *dukkha. Dukkha* is usually translated as "suffering," but the word is better translated as "existential estrangement." The Pali word *dukkha* refers literally to an axle that is off-center with respect to its wheel or to a bone that has slipped out of its socket.[15] Therefore *dukkha* implies an existential estrangement, an estrangement of relationship. Since life in a state of *dukkha,* or distorted relationship, is in constant motion and process, it expresses itself as pain and suffering, just as a leg whose tibia has slipped out of its socket is painful when it moves. That is why the life of sin is a life of suffering. Moreover, this existential estrangement disrupts the natural process of creativity in the world. When the wheel is out of alignment with its axis, it turns with difficulty or not at all.

By sin, or existential estrangement, the normal activity of God is disrupted and the harmony between creator and creature or between the change and that which changes is upset. Sin is the disruption of changing process and becoming. Sin is nothing but humanity's desire to *be* rather than to *become*; it is our unwillingness to change. This desire to *be* is one of the strongest inclinations of all creatures. It is expressed as nostalgia, which is usually defined as longing for the past but might be more accurately defined as futile unwillingness to change. We have no choice but to change. We are sojourners and pilgrims toward the never attained "not yet." In the never-ending process of change we as creatures are born and die, grow and decay. The desire to *be*—to remain unchanged in the moving stream of life—is the existential estrangement, or sin. To overcome this desire to *be*—this clutch at stasis—is the goal or salvation. Thus the work of salvation is the restoration of normal creativity.

Salvation, then, means to follow the way of change without nostalgia. When Jesus said, "I am the Way," he was referring to the way of change. By calling us to him, Jesus calls us to be one with the change, which is the source of all changes. To those who want to *be*, or to remain, Jesus said, "Follow me," which is the core of his message. "Follow me" is Christ's unconditional command. One cannot look back. One cannot even go back to bury one's father. Jesus said, "Follow me, and leave the dead to bury their own dead" (Matt. 8:22). Jesus is the way of change, which is directed to the new creation. To be in the way of change, that is, in Christ, we must give up trying to establish our security on *be*ing. We must be ready always to become and to change in the direction that Jesus leads. We must not ask: "Are you running with me, Jesus?" but rather: "Am I running with you, Jesus?" Karl Barth defines Christ as the archetype of a person to become the model of what a person should be. Jesus said, "I am the Way," the way of truth and change, and because he is our way, he calls us to follow. He is *yang* and we are *yin*. It is *yang's* function to act and initiate and *yin's* to respond and follow. Christ is creative because of *yang;* we must be receptive because of *yin.* Our only proper action, as *yin,* is to respond.

By our response, however, we become creative, because *yin* becomes *yang* by response and *yang* becomes *yin* by creation. Thus we become active by our inaction, creative by our response, and joyful by our suffering. It is a paradox of Christian experience. As Paul says, "We are treated as impostors, and yet are true; as unknown, and yet well known; as dying, and behold we live; as punished, and yet not killed; as sorrowful, yet always rejoicing; as poor, yet making many rich; as having nothing, and yet possessing everything" (2 Cor. 6:8-10). This idea is also expressed in the *Tao te ching,* the Taoist Scripture, which says, "The Way is gained by daily loss, loss upon loss until at last comes rest. By letting go, it all gets done; the world is won by those who let it go! But when you try and try, the world is then beyond the winning."[16] The way of *yin* is to gain by losing itself, or, in Paul's words, "It is no longer I who live, but Christ who lives in me" (Gal. 2:2). By responding to Christ's call to follow him, we cause him to act in us, as *yang* acts in *yin.* That is how "by letting go, it all gets done." The change changes us. Or, in other words, God rules us.

By letting go, our way becomes his way and his way becomes ours. That is the secret of the way of change, the *tao.* Christ triumphed by loss of self. By enduring total defeat in crucifixion, he gained complete victory in resurrection. To give in full is to receive in full. Certainly receiving is giving and giving is receiving. Lao Tzu says, "The movement of the way is a return; in weakness lies its strength."[17] And Jesus' teaching that the last shall be first and the exalted shall be humbled is identical in meaning. All phenomena, upon reaching their ultimate, must revert toward their antitheses. At noon the day begins to wane; at midnight night begins to lighten and day to dawn. By letting go of our *being*—of what we *are* at some finite moment—we become one with the way of change and transformation, and that is the way of salvation.

To be saved means to be part of the process of change and

transformation brought about by the power of the change. Salvation is the harmony between the change and the changing or between the creator and the creature. It is like the harmony of *yin* and *yang*. Christ died not to anguish the world but to reconcile it to its creator. As Paul said, ''God was in Christ reconciling the world to himself, not counting their trespasses against them, and entrusting to us the message of reconciliation'' (2 Cor. 5:19). Salvation does not mean the subjugation of the world by the divine. Rather it means the harmonization of the world with the way of God's creative process of change. It is the process of reconciliation between creator and creature or between the change and the changing world. It is the harmony of *yin* and *yang* which makes all things in peace. Thus to be saved means to be in harmony with the principle of change, which by the process of creation makes all things.

To be in harmony with changing process means to change. Therefore, as Paul said, ''If anyone is in Christ, he is a new creation; the old has passed away, behold the new has come'' (2 Cor. 5:17). The new creation Paul speaks of is new to the creature, but to the creator it is simply a *re*newal of what has already been. The new, or renewed, creation is essentially the same but existentially different from the old creation. The process of divine creativity, then, is a process of constant renewal of what has already been. That is what Ecclesiastes meant by saying, ''There is nothing new under the sun.'' Things new to us are not new to the creator. Divine creativity, which is perfectly manifested in Christ, is the power of renewal through the constant interplay of *yin* and *yang*. This interplay makes renewal possible, and renewal makes creativity possible.

In the Book of Changes there are sixty-four archetypes that are continually renewed to create new existences. They are essentially unchanging, even though they are manifest as many different forms in existence. Thus the change does not create anything really new but renews the old. In this renewing process, that is, the creative process, new existences are born of already existing essences. Creativity, in this sense, is never a progress toward novelty. As the Great Commentary says, ''Change and transformation are images of progress and regression.''[18] Advance necessarily leads to retrogression. As *yin* grows, *yang* decays; as *yang* grows, *yin* decays. Nothing can progress or develop indefinitely. A belief in infinite progression in history is contrary to the cyclic movement of time described in the *I ching*. In the world of relativity and change we cannot claim that history moves always and only forward.

In fact, salvation history includes both progression and retrogression. The end of time, or *eschaton*, must not be understood as the ultimate termination of history. *Eschaton* is the end of the old as well as the beginning of the new, that is, the renewal of the old. As Jacob says, "Eschatology is a return to the beginning; but with something additional which was absent at the first creation."[19] Every day is the end of time and beginning of renewed time. The end of the world in the New Testament does not mean the absolute end but the end of the old and the beginning of the new world through the power of renewal. It is the coming to an end of a cosmic span of change. Everything has its own span of change. When the span ends it is renewed. That is why we see in the ending of the world the images of a new heaven and a new earth. When the Last Judgment is over, the new heaven and new earth appear. "Then I saw a new heaven and a new earth; for the first heaven and the first earth have passed away, and the sea was no more. And I saw the holy city, the new Jerusalem, coming down out of heaven from God, prepared as a bride adorned for her husband" (Rev. 21:1–2). The new heaven and new earth and the new Jerusalem are symbols of renewal. They are not essentially new but are renewals of the old heaven and earth. Thus, in essence, ending is the beginning of renewal. In this process of renewal, that is, in the process of salvation, the world is in constant change and transformation. Christ shows us the way to be in this process of renewal and becoming, for he is the pioneer of our salvation.

Christ is the pioneer of our salvation, because he is "the first born of all creation." He is the origin of creative process toward which salvation history moves, for salvation is a process of returning to the origin of creation. "He is before all things, and in him all things hold together" (Col. 1:17). In other words; he is the center and origin of all creative processes and of all their manifestations. This center is the seed or origin of all creation.

CHRIST AS THE CENTER OF THE CREATIVE PROCESS

Christ as the center of the cosmic process is analogous to the Indian symbol of the cosmic center, the mythic Mt. Meru, which is also the symbol of Brahman, Hinduism's name for ultimate reality. Here Christ, as the symbol of the cosmic center is parallel to Brahman, the Hindu notion of the ultimate reality, who also symbolizes the cosmic center. He is the center of every creative process, for the cosmic center includes all macrocosmic as well as microcosmic centers. Therefore the cosmic Christ also represents the center of the human soul and the axis of human life. As St. John of the Cross says, "The center of the soul *is* God."[20] Just as a wheel's axis is empty, Christ as the center of existence is empty; he is *śūnyatā*, or nonbeing, which is the origin of all creative becoming.

Christ is the divine reality. In him, that is, in the core of every creative process, all distinctions disappear. In Christ object and subject, inner and outer, good and evil become indistinguishable. In the center of the changing process, which is Christ, not only *all* things but all times—past, present, and future—come together. This undifferentiated time is eternity, in which the beginning is also the ending and the ending is also the beginning. Therefore to be in the center of changing process is also to be in eternity. By saying, "I am the Alpha and Omega, the first and the last, the beginning and the end" (Rev. 22:13), Jesus meant that he is eternal. In the primordial center he is one "who is and who was and who is to come" (Rev. 1:8). He is then the symbol of eternal change, which is the perfect manifestation of change itself.

Christ as the symbol of the concentric point of every creative process embraces all dimensions of time and space. To return to this primordial origin is in a way to be in union with the eternal reality. In it humanity is free from the illusion of *māyā* and the bondage of sin. For the individual who has "found"—or understood—the center, the wheel of life stops turning. At the center of existence humanity is totally detached from the phenomenal world, yet totally attached to the real world. Thus to be in Christ means to be simultaneously attached and detached. Paul says that in Christ we are not of the world but in the world. Because Christ occupies the center of creative process, where *māyā* and sin do not exist, salvation is in him.

DIVINITY AND HUMANITY OF CHRIST

As the primordial origin of the creative process, Christ is also both divine and human. In this center the distinction between man and God disappears. This continuum between humanity and divinity is the real meaning of incarnation. Because he occupies the center of the cosmic process, the incarnate Christ becomes the focus of the universal aspiration and goal of the whole world. The existence and destiny of everything in the world, personal or impersonal, has its source in Christ. Christ as the primordial center of the creative process is the perfect incarnation of the infinite in the finite world; he is human and divine in the fullest sense. He is fully divine because he is fully human. He is a perfect man because he is a perfect God. His human perfection is manifested in his friendship and brotherhood to all humankind. As a true brother he shows us the way to the Father, and as a true friend he lays down his life for us. He is a man for others, standing in the place where others must stand but cannot. He is also divine in a perfect sense because he occupies the center of divine creativity. In him the power of the change is manifested perfectly. He is in perfect harmony with the process of the change. Because of this perfect harmony, his will and the will of God are one and inseparable. That is what Jesus meant by saying "Believe in me that I am in the Father and the Father in me" (John 14:11).

The relationship between Christ's divinity and humanity is like the relationship between *yin* and *yang*. Just as *yang* cannot exist without *yin* nor *yin* without *yang*, the humanity of Jesus cannot exist without the divinity of Christ nor the divinity of Christ without the humanity of Jesus. "In him God is not separated from man nor man from God. They are in complementary relationship. He is God because of man: He is man because of God."[21] In Jesus as the Christ man and God are in perfect harmony. Jesus' divinity does not preclude his humanity but rather presupposes it, just as *yang* presupposes the existence of *yin*. Furthermore, perfect humanity presupposes perfect divinity. In his perfect complementarity of divine and human, or of the change and the changing, he is both perfect man and perfect God. Being the symbol of perfect harmony between the change and the changing, Jesus Christ is the ultimate reality of change and transformation.

As the basis of creativity Christ is also the perfect symbol of the divine nature. He is the perfect symbol of the creator who is the eternal subject, unknown to us. He transcends the division between subject and object and all other categorizations by which we express our understanding of reality. God as creator is the background of all process and becoming. Christ as the primordial origin of creative energy becomes the mediator between God as creator and humanity as creature. Christ as a mediator functions symbolically. "Thus the symbol functions as a mediator which can transform subject to object. However, this does not mean that God is no longer revealing Himself as the Subject. He is the Subject of us always, but He is seen as the object of our knowledge when we see Him through the symbol."[22]

Christ is a perfect symbol, not only because we see God in him perfectly, but because we see ourselves in him perfectly. In him "Very God does indeed energize in Very Man."[23] Because we see ourselves perfectly in him, he also becomes the perfect symbol of humanity. We become subjects of God by participating in this perfect symbol of God and man. As a wheel's axis is empty, Christ's mind is still, reflecting like a mirror every impulse of the change. His heart is unadultered and his attitude unadorned. He is like the *p'o,* the virgin block of wood untouched by human artifice, which is the Taoist symbol of perfection. He is like the children whom he described as "belonging to the kingdom of heaven." His purity of heart, sincerity of conviction, simplicity of life, and conformability with change are attributes of the perfect symbol of both creator and creature. Christ is present to us as a perfect symbol of the reality of God's creativity and humanity's response to it; he is *yang* to humanity's *yin* and *yin* to the creator's *yang*. Because everything owes its existence and renewal to the continual interaction of *yang* and *yin*, Jesus is the perfect symbol of "both-and," which is the normative description of ultimate reality.

THE CRUCIFIXION AND RESURRECTION OF CHRIST

The most vivid reminders of Christ's living presence as the perfect symbol of change are life and death. The perfect symbol of death is Jesus' crucifixion, because Jesus is the perfect symbol of every process, including death and life. The perfect symbol of life is the renewal of life in Jesus' resurrection. Just as death presupposes life, crucifixion presupposes resurrection. In early Indian scriptures Shiva appeared as the destroyer of life, but later he acquired regenerative powers as well, because renewal presupposes the destruction of the old. Like Shiva, Christ symbolizes both the destruction and the renewal of life. Christ's death is not symbolic of the total annihilation of life but of its existential negation. Thus the essential nature, or archetype, of humanity is not thereby extinguished. Christ's resurrection is then the renewal of the archetype in a form existentially different but essentially the same. Since crucifixion and resurrection act upon the same essence, or archetype, they are existentially not contradictory but ultimately complementary. Christ's resurrection is not the conquest of death but the fulfillment of life, and his crucifixion was necessary for that fulfillment. What is to be renewed must first die. Thus Jesus as the perfect symbol of the change unites both decay and growth or death and resurrection in the process of constant change and transformation.

Crucifixion and resurrection represent the matrices of all changes and transformations in the world. They symbolize winter and spring, evening and morning, rest and motion. Crucifixion and resurrection are *yin* and *yang*, the gateways to all changes, and they occur in all things, because all things change. If crucifixion and resurrection are common to all things, how are Jesus' crucifixion and resurrection unique?

Death on the cross was not uncommon in the Roman world,

nor was the belief in resurrection throughout the Near and Middle East.[24] Jesus' followers fully expected to die and be raised again to life as he had been. Jesus' crucifixion and resurrection are unique, not because they happened to him, but because they became the primordial symbol of all changing. They also became the primordial symbols of Christian life. As Paul says, "For if we have been united with him in a death like his, we shall certainly be united with him in a resurrection like his" (Rom. 6:5), and, "The death he died he died to sin, once for all, but the life he lives he lives to God. So you also must consider yourselves dead to sin and alive to God in Christ Jesus" (Rom. 6:11). Jesus' resurrection became the primordial symbol of Christianity's renewing power engendering a saving process that consists in a return to original creativity. As Moltmann says, "Christianity stands or falls with the reality of the raising of Jesus from the dead by God. In the New Testament there is no faith that does not start a priori with the resurrection of Jesus."[25] Jesus' resurrection is distinguished from all other forms of life renewal by its primordial symbolism, through which everyone can experience the renewal of life and enter into the creative process. In it we may take part in the renewing process of change and understand the eternal change in the midst of a changing world.

Notes

1. Paul Tillich, *Systematic Theology* (Chicago: University of Chicago Press, 1957), vol. 2, *Existence and the Christ*, p. 146.

2. This concept of salvation as the recapitulation of original creation was originally proposed by Irenaeus and came to be accepted widely, especially by the so-called Lundensian theology.

3. Emil Brunner, *The Christian Doctrine of God*, trans. Olive Wyon (Philadelphia: Westminster Press, 1950), p. 217.

4. Ibid., p. 232.

5. Thorlief Boman, *Hebrew Thought Compared with Greek*, trans. Jules J. Moreau (London: SCM Press, 1960), p. 58.

6. Ibid., p. 60.

7. Ibid., p. 68.

8. John's prologue, especially his use of a cosmogony as the basis of his message of salvation, is often thought to reflect the Hellenistic ideas as expressed in the *Heremetica*. This does not, however, eliminate the fundamental connection between the Old and New Testament meanings of "the Word."

9. C. K. Barrett, *The Gospel According to St. John: An Introduction with Commentary and Notes on the Greek Text* (London: SPCK, 1960), p. 131.

10. Alan Richardson, *An Introduction to the Theology of the New Testament* (New York: Harper and Row, 1958), p. 156.

11. The phrase "image of God" is used in the Greek Old Testament to refer to the divine wisdom (Wisd. 7:26). See also S. Radhakrishnan, *Religion in a Changing World* (London: George Allen and Unwin, 1967), p. 107.

12. D. T. Suzuki, *Essays in Zen Buddhism,* Third Series (London: Rider and Co., 1958), p. 254.

13. Brunner, *Christian Doctrine of God,* p. 232.

14. See chapter 2.

15. See Huston Smith, *The Religions of Man* (New York: Harper and Row, 1958), p. 99.

16. *Tao te ching,* trans. by R. S. Blakney (New York: New American Library, 1955), ch. 48.

17. Ibid., ch. 40.

18. *Ta chuan,* sec. I, ch. 2.

19. Edmond Jacob, *Theology of the Old Testament* (New York: Harper and Brothers, 1958), p. 142.

20. R. C. Zaehner, *Mysticism Sacred and Profane* (New York and London: Oxford University Press, 1961), p. 137.

21. J. Y. Lee, "The Yin-Yang Way of Thinking," *International Review of Mission,* July 1971, p. 370.

22. J. Y. Lee, *The I: A Christian Concept of Man* (New York: Philosophical Library, 1971), p. 71.

23. Norman Pittenger, *God in Process* (London: SCM, 1967), p. 70.

24. Osiris in Egypt, Tammuz in Babylon, and Attis in Asia Minor exemplify ancient Near Eastern beliefs in resurrection. Even though the manner of resurrection differs in different traditions, we can say that the idea of resurrection was widely held in the New Testament time. There is some truth in what Moltmann said: "Christianity differs from the Hellenistic view for it participates not in perfect resurrection but in the present or the future hope" (Jürgen Moltmann, *Theology of Hope,* New York: Harper and Row, 1967, p. 161).

25. Jürgen Moltmann, *Theology of Hope,* p. 165.

CHAPTER VI

THE SPIRIT
AND THE UNITY OF CHANGE:
THE HOLY SPIRIT AND THE TRINITY

THE MEANING OF SPIRIT

The word "spirit" (*ruach* in Hebrew, *pneuma* in Greek) is synonymous with "wind" and "breath," but the Bible implies so many variant meanings, depending on context, that a brief etymology would aid our understanding of the word. The term *ruach* seems originally to have meant "the air, which manifests itself in two forms—that of the wind in nature and of breath in living beings."[1] The Sanskrit word *prāna*, whose literal meaning is "breath," seems to correspond to *ruach*. In later Vedic literature it denotes "the breath of life," hence "spirit" or "soul." In Hindu literature of the post-Vedic period "*prāna*" denotes one of the five "winds" of the body, residing in the heart and responsible for life.[2] In the Old Testament *ruach* came to be associated with the active power of God's creativity. In the New Testament it is closely associated with the Son and the Father, though Paul seems to identify spirit with the Son alone.[3]

John 4:24 relates the concept of spirit to the concept of God briefly and unequivocally: "God is spirit." Substituting the original meaning of *ruach* for "spirit" in this statement leads us to the conclusion that God is both wind and the breath of his creature. I believe this to be a profound insight. We have so emphasized our personal relationship with God that we have almost forgotten that God is also the creator and sustainer of the world. If God is wind as well as breath, then he is impersonal or nonpersonal as well as personal. The inclusive God cannot be expressed by the "either-or" category of description, only by the "both-and" category. If, as John says, God is spirit, then spirit is also both personal and impersonal. In "both-and" terms, then, what is the spirit?

In the Bible the spirit as wind is closely associated with God. The wind represents the power of God in nature. It drove back the sea and permitted the Israelites to escape from Egypt (Exod. 14:21, 15:8). The wind dried up the springs (Hos. 14:15) but also brought the clouds to give rain to the plants (1 Kings 18:45). Wind is the force that controls the destiny of nature. God is manifested in nature and rules nature as the wind that he has created. The wind, which is an invisible force controlling nature, denotes the power of nature's inner self. It is the inner presence of all things, the power that makes them grow or decay, expand or contract.

The spirit as wind in nature is, in other words, the power of change, since the principle of growth and decay or expansion and contraction is subject to this power. The power of change is the essence of all existence: It is the power of production and repro- duction as well as growth and decay. It is the inner essence, which cannot be grasped but is known in its manifestation. Flowers and trees grow and decay, yet we do not see the power working in them, only their manifest growth and decay. But the power of change, or the spirit in nature, cannot be understood by observation of the creatures in which it is manifested. It is not only the invisible force that creates visible changes, but the very subject of everything manifest in the world. In other words, the spirit in nature is matter unmanifested, and matter is the spirit manifested. Spirit and matter are in essence one but in existence separate and disparate. Spirit can become matter and matter can become spirit, just as energy can become matter and matter can become energy under certain conditions.

SPIRIT AND MATTER

The continuity between spiritual power and its material man- ifestation is clearly expressed in the story of creation. Before earth and heaven were created, at the origin of creation, there was the spirit of God, or the wind, moving over the primeval water (Gen. 1:2). As Jacob says, "The spirit is God himself in creation."[4] To separate the spirit from the material entity is to postulate a false dualism in Judeo-Christianity. Since everything, whether spiritual or material, comes from God, there can be no essential differentiation between matter and spirit; their differentiation is existential or phenomenal. Therefore spirit is the essence of all things manifested and things are objectifications of spirit. In this sense, spirit alone is the subject of all existence of all material manifestation. Thus correctly interpreted, spirit and matter are beyond duality.

By stripping the Judeo-Christian worldview of its false dualism, we come to see how much it resembles Indian and Chinese views of the world and God. In Hinduism the world of matter *separated from the spirit of Brahman, or reality,* is considered illusory, and this illusory world is commonly called *māyā. Māyā,* "illusion," is not material entity as such, as is often mistakenly assumed in the West, but only material entity divorced from Brahman. To separate anything from Brahman, or spirit, is to make it unreal. Hinduism, particularly the Vedantic tradition, which is radically monistic, emphasizes the essential insepara-bleness of spirit and matter and conceives the world as the actual manifestation of Brahman and Brahman as the subject of the manifested world. Brahman, or spiritual reality, or the spirit of God, is the eternal subject of all things.

The Bhagavad Gita, one of Hinduism's most popular scriptures, affirms the interdependence of the spiritual and material nature, depicting Brahman as the womb of all things: "My womb is the great Brahman; in it I plant the germ. Thence comes the origin of all beings."[5] Since the material nature has its origin in God, it partakes also of divinity. So God has a double nature, a "lower," or material, and a "higher," or spiritual.[6] "Earth, water, fire, wind, ether, thought-organ, consciousness, and I-faculty: thus is divided My material nature, eight-fold. This is [My] lower [nature]. But know My other nature, higher than that. It is the soul by which this world is sustained."[7] Primordial matter, or *prakriti,* certainly does not originate independently of Brahman.

It is God's own, whose essence is the spirit. Thus the whole material universe is regarded as the manifestation of his spiritual nature, which sustains the material nature. Since God is ultimately one, his material nature is simultaneously his spiritual nature. In the highest reality the two natures are identical. According to the Heart Sutra of Mahayana Buddhism, nirvana and samsara, or the spiritual and material natures, are identical.[8] Ignorance and illusion result from the false dualism that separates matter from spirit. In God one is in all and all is in one.

The *I ching* too expresses a monistic worldview: Everything, spiritual and material, comes from the interplay of *yin* and *yang*. The distinction between *yin* and *yang* is not absolute; neither can exist without the other. Even though they are distinctive in their existences, they are essentially one and undifferentiated, mutually inclusive and interdependent. This undifferentiated unity of *yin* and *yang*, which exists in the change, is the ultimate source of all things. Thus the *I ching*, like the Judeo-Christian, Vedantic, and Zen Buddhist traditions, is essentially monistic. In Chinese cosmology the *yang* force is spirit and *yin* force is matter. The relationship between spirit and matter is, then, the relationship between *yin* and *yang*. Since *yin* and *yang* are mutually interdependent and complementary, spirit and matter are also essentially inseparable. Since change occurs through the interplay of *yin* and *yang*, God as change itself is active in both spiritual and material realms. The separation of spirit from matter is impossible in the ultimate reality, because spirit and matter are ultimately one.

SPIRIT AS LIFE AND POWER

The Hebrew term *ruach*, whose translation as "wind," or the power of change in nature, we have discussed above, also denotes the breath of life, especially in humankind. Breath is clearly associated with life. According to the Upanishads, "Life is the breathing spirit. The breathing spirit, verily is life. . . . For, as long as the breathing spirit remains in this body, so long is there life."[9] Since life and breath observably cease together, it is natural to assume that breath is the power that gives life. The Old Testament refers repeatedly to the life-giving power as God's breath (Gen. 6:17; Num. 16:22; Ps. 104:29; Eccles. 3:1; Isa. 37:6, etc.). In the Yahwistic narration of the creation of humankind, "The Lord God formed man of dust from the ground, and breathed into his nostrils the breath of life; and man became a living being" (Gen. 2:7). Here the breath of life, anthropomorphically envisaged to come from the mouth of God, gives life to man. In the Elohist narrative of creation, the breath of life is identically used with the image of God: "So God created man in his own image, in the image of God he created him; male and female he created them" (Gen. 1:27). Both the image of God and the breath of life represent the spirit which gives the power of life.

In the Upanishads, Brahma, the creator, is identified with *prāna*, breath: "Brahma, verily, is the breath of life *(prāna)*."[10] Similar usages occur throughout the Old and New Testaments. For example, "I will pour my spirit upon your descendants, and my blessing on your offspring. They shall spring up like grass amid waters, like willows by flowing streams" (Isa. 44:3). In the New Testament the disciples proclaim their belief that God will pour out his spirit upon all flesh (Acts 2:16–18; 10:45; Rom. 5:5; Gal. 4:6, etc.). The spirit, *pneuma,* which is also breath, is particularly remarked as the life-giving power in the Synoptic accounts of Christ's birth (Matt. 1:18,20; Luke 1:15,35,41; 2:25,27). In the Fourth Gospel, however, Jesus proclaims the future coming of the Spirit (John 14:16–18,26; 15:26; 16:7–14) to carry out the work of Christ.

There are many other New Testament references to God's spirit working in the life of the church, and in almost all of these the spirit, as the breath of God, represents the power of giving life or renewing life. In speaking of the life of the church, the New Testament authors describe the spirit as the power that gives new life: He is the Spirit of life (John 6:23; 1 Cor. 15:45), who breathes life into the new creation (John 20:22; Rev. 11:11). Though spirit, in the sense of breath, has various connotations, its central meaning is, as Tillich suggests, the power of life: "Where there is breath, there is the power of life; where it vanishes, the power of life vanishes."[11] The practice of meditation or yoga has led eastern mystics to the identical conclusion. During meditation or yoga all conscious functions of the mind and the senses can be suspended for a comparatively long time, but not breathing. "As long as there is breath, there is life."[12] Breath is a metaphor for life and a symbol of all the forces that sustain life. "Thus breathing becomes a vehicle of spiritual experience, the mediator between body and mind."[13]

The breath not only gives life but renews it through its power that is the Spirit. This power inspired the prophets to preach the Word of God, united people in his church through ecstatic experiences like the descent of the Spirit at Pentecost, witnessed for Christ both in individuals and in the community, and appeared in many different forms under different conditions. Therefore the spirit as the power of life is not limited to any particular mode of appearance. The spirit is manifested in an infinite variety of forms and styles that may be, and in fact often are, unrecognized by humanity. Tillich says that the spirit is the all-embracing symbol whose known presence is the answer to the ambiguity of our lives.[14] It cannot be limited to places, words, institutions, or offices designated as sacred by humanity.

It is not even valid to distinguish, as Tillich does, between the spirit of God and the spirit of man, because this implies a limitation on God's spiritual presence in the world.[15] But God's presence in the world is not limited, because the spirit as wind or breath is present in all things living and nonliving. Just as the Upanishads make no distinction between the cosmic God, Brahman, and the individual soul, Ātman, there is no real distinction between the spirit of God and the spirit of man. Because the spirit of God is all-penetrating and all-present, all things are related as microcosms of the same macrocosm. The spirit that is in humanity is also in animals, trees, and stones. In essence spirit is one and undifferentiated, and its omnipresence is the necessary condition of monotheism. Because spirit is in all things and all conditions of time and place, the world is alive and changing constantly. The spirit is, then, the power of change that renews all things, and therefore "all dynamic qualities, all that causes movement, change or transformation, reveals the nature of *prāna* (spirit)."[16]

SPIRIT AS INNER ESSENCE

Spirit manifested as wind is the inner essence of all things nonhuman. It is the eternal subject of the variegated, manifest world. It is therefore the power of unity as well as disunity, integration as well as disintegration, growth as well as decay, expansion as well as contraction, birth as well as death. It is the inner power that controls external appearances and forms. It is the essence of existence, and the potentiality of all possibilities. It is like the archetype of all existence. Yet spirit and material existences are neither dichotomous nor separable. They are in essence an undifferentiated continuum, differentiated only in existence. They are mutually interdependent, just as *yin* and *yang* are mutually inclusive and complementary.

Likewise, the spirit manifested as the breath of God is the inner essence and eternal subject of humanity. It is what makes us as we are—human and alive. In sum, spirit as God's breath is the essence of humanity, and spirit as wind is the essence of the cosmos. Though the spirit cannot be known by us except in manifestation, it is active in us as subject, or "in the form of human inwardness."[17] It is the wellspring of our existence and our action. We must recognize its omnipresence, by which it unites us with everything in the world. Since our inner essence is God's spirit in us, responding to God means responding to our inner essence, the subject of our humanity. This inner presence is, therefore, present at all times for our response. It is an active and dynamic energy with power to reshape and renew life. Paul reminds us of this by asking: "Do you not know that your body is a temple of the Holy Spirit within you, which you have from God?" (1 Cor. 6:19). Likewise Jeremiah, speaking for the Lord to his people, says: "I will put my law within them, and I will write it upon their hearts; and I will be their God, and they shall be my people" (Jer. 31:33). The spirit is present in us as innermost self, the soul or center of our existence. Like Ātman, the soul in all things that is our subject though we are unconscious of it,[18] the spirit never becomes the object of our knowledge. It does not reveal itself to our consciousness but is the wellspring of our conscious selves.

SPIRIT AS *YIN*

The spirit as subject of our humanity is hidden from our active minds, because it is essentially the *yin,* or receptive, aspect of divine creativity. Its receptive quality permits humans freedom of decision and action. If the spirit were the *yang* aspect of divine creativity, human beings could have no conscious free will. Although the spirit is the *yin* aspect of divine creativity, it represents the subject, that is, the *yang* aspect of human life. In other words, the spirit is *yin* in essence but becomes *yang* in existence by virtue of being the subject of human existence. Even as the subject of existence it retains its *yin* qualities of receptiveness, quiescence, and femininity.[19]

Pittenger gives a helpful illustration of the *yin* character of the spirit: "The writer of a devotional book which I read many years ago made an interesting point about the Holy Spirit, when he described it as 'the humblest person in the Godhead. ' . . .One could put it by saying that the Holy Spirit is very frequently quite unrecognized because in fact he works 'anonymously' among us and in the world."[20] The spirit is anonymous because of its essential *yin* character. Therefore the spirit as our subject does not dominate us but waits upon our response. God as the spirit is patient even to the point of suffering in order to allow us the freedom of our conscious response.

The Holy Spirit is in this respect analogous to the Taoist *tao,* which is characterized by the receptiveness of change. Like the Holy Spirit, *tao* is patient and yielding. It changes, without intent, like buds opening. It accomplishes everything by inaction. Such spontaneous activity is the way of *tao.* Lao Tzu says, "Tao invariably takes no action, and yet there is nothing left undone. . . . All things will transform spontaneously."[21] Likewise the spirit becomes the wellspring of active life. It is active without action. This spontaneity is the origin of our freedom. Our true freedom comes from our response to our inwardness, to the spirit in us saying "Follow me." That is what Jesus meant by saying, "If you continue in my word, you are truly my disciples, and you will know the truth, and the truth will make you free" (John 8:31–32). To follow him is to be one with the spirit, and to be united with the spirit is to be free indeed. To follow him is to renounce ourselves and the power of self-objectifying process. Renouncing this power means giving up the security of being in order to follow him. It means giving up the desire to remain static in the midst of change and transformation. The archetype of humanity, which is the spirit, is the power of change that changes all changing phenomena.

Thus to yield ourselves to the spirit means to change according to the change that is the source of all change and creativity. To be in harmony with that change is true freedom. To be free indeed is to be unconscious of self. To be unconscious of self is to be free of the power of objectification. When we are free of this power, we can be creative and spontaneous, because we are of the spirit. To be ruled by the spirit means to be one with the spirit. When oneness with the spirit is attained, the spirit need no longer function as the *yang* of human existence; being one with humanity, the spirit then resumes its essential nature, that is, the *yin* of divine creativity, to fulfill the ultimate goal of God the creator. When our spirit, united with the spirit of God, becomes a part of divine creativity, divine harmony ensues. This divine harmony, which is restored through our response to the spirit of God, implies complete harmony between the change and changing phenomena. Complete harmony between the change and changing phenomena may be the kingdom of God on a cosmic scale.

PROBLEMS OF THE TRINITY

Let us now consider the meanings of the relationships among the names of God in the Trinity: the Word (or the Son), the Spirit (or the Holy Spirit), and the Creator (or the Father). These relationships constitute one of the most difficult problems in the history of Christian thought. The trinitarian doctrine of God established by the early church has been seriously challenged in our time. Karl Barth accepts the traditional doctrine of the Trinity but alters personal categories to ontic categories and the three

Persons into three modes of being (*Seinsweisen*). But this is modalistic heresy, even though Barth stresses the simultaneous manifestation of divine modes of being.

Brunner rejects the traditional formula of the Trinity as the church's defensive reaction against Jewish monotheism and pagan polytheism. Though he calls the traditional trinitarian doctrine an intellectual indulgence of the early church fathers, Brunner proceeds to formulate his own Trinity, in which he rejects the traditional *tres personae* and *una substantia*, the former because it may lead to the notion of a tritheistic God and the latter because its neutral, metaphysical connotations render God impersonal. For *tres personae* Brunner substitutes three names of God, and for *una substantia*, one love. He defends the functional subordinationism as the biblical idea of the Trinity, but he sets up the irrevocable and absolute orders of divine manifestation in terms of "one after another."[22]

Bultmann has generally ignored the doctrine of the Trinity. Tillich rejects, humorously but utterly, Barth's postulation of the Trinity as the compendium of Christian faith: "It was a mistake of Barth to start his Prolegomena with what, so to speak, are the Postlegomena, the doctrine of the Trinity. It could be said that in his system this doctrine falls from heaven, the heaven of an unmediated biblical and ecclesiastical authority."[23] Tillich emphasizes the priority of human situations as the conditioning factors of divine manifestations. He says, "The trinitarian symbolism must be understood as an answer to the questions implied in man's predicament."[24] By denouncing the Barthian absolutism of divine priority, Tillich sets up another absolutism of his theological method of correlation, which prevents the spontaneity of the divine spirit.

The work of these men can help us understand the relationship among the three divine symbols. The terms used to describe the divine nature and the order of manifestation of the three forms of God are important to our understanding of the trinitarian God. But the fundamental problem in understanding the divine Trinity is neither the definition of terms nor the order of divine manifestations but our way of thinking. In other words, our way of thinking, the "either-or" way of thinking that categorizes things absolutely, is fundamentally responsible for the countless controversies on the doctrine of the Trinity. If we transcend our habit of absolute categorization, we may be able to resolve many problems related to the trinitarian question. Therefore, let us first consider the modes of thought that have created the trinitarian concept of God.

"Either-or" thinking, based on the Aristotelian axiom of the "excluded middle," cannot describe God, since God transcends the differentiation between subject and object, essence and existence, transcendence and immanence. By "either-or" logic God must be *either* one *or* three. He cannot be *both* one *and* three at the same time. But to describe the divine Trinity requires the most inclusive category of description, that is, the "both-and," or *yin-yang*, way of thinking, which derives from the idea of change. Using this way of thinking we may be able to resolve some of the problems in the doctrine of the Trinity.

In the previous chapter we described the change, the "begetter of all begetting," as the Creator. The Son as the Word, when considered from the perspective of the Creator, is the power of creation, or the center of the creative process. The Word to the Hebrew mind is active and creative energy, which is analogous to *yang*. Since *yang* is a creative force, we can use *yang* to express the Word as the creative power of God. The Spirit is *yin* in character, as we have stated, because it "is concerned primarily with *response* to the outgoing revelatory and redemptive action of God."[25] On the other hand, "the outgoing revelatory and redemptive action of God" is unquestionably identified with the Word, or creativity (*yang*). There appears to be, then, a correlation between the *yin-yang* way of thinking and the divine symbols of the Trinity. The Creator (or the Father) is correlated with the change, the Word (or the Son) with *yang*, and the Spirit (or the Holy Spirit) with *yin*. Can this correlation explain the heart of Christian paradoxes: "the threeness in one and oneness in three?"

Since we have substituted for the biblical symbols of Creator, Word, and Spirit the metaphysical symbols of change, *yang*, and *yin*, we must consider how the latter are related to one another in terms of "threeness in one and oneness in three." The change as the begetter of all begetting is the source of all creativity. The basic constituents of the change, however, are *yin* and *yang*. The interaction of *yin* and *yang* makes the change possible. In this respect the interplay of *yin* and *yang* are identical with the change. Nevertheless, the primacy of the change to these primordial forces is unquestioned, because the change is the begetter of all begetting. It has primacy over all changing process. Just as the Creator is the basis of the creative act of the Word, the change is the basis of *yin* and *yang*. The change, however, has only functional primacy; ontologically the change is *yin-yang*. Between *yin* and *yang* there can be no relationship of priority, since they are mutually dependent. To attempt an irreversible order of Word and Spirit—in which the early churchmen and even some contemporaries doggedly persist—is mistaken and doomed to failure. To assume a necessary sequence of divine manifestations is to limit the spontaneity of divine activity and to presuppose static ontology. Sequence is important in the deterministic and mechanistic understanding of being, which is governed by the strict principle of cause and effect, but in the changing and organic world of becoming, movements are often not in sequence but in contingency. Divine manifestations are not sequential but simultaneously spontaneous.

THE TRINITY IN "BOTH-AND" LOGIC

Now let us consider in what sense the divine manifestations can be "three in one and one in three." In the "either-or" way of thinking, in which categories are differentiated absolutely, "three in one and one in three" is incomprehensible. The fallacy in "either-or" logic consists in treating one aspect of the whole in isolation from the whole. But the Creator cannot be understood in isolation from the Word and the Spirit. In the fable of the blind men and the elephant, the elephant as a whole proved not to resemble any of its parts. Discussing the Trinity in Aristotelian terms much resembles the blind men's visit to the elephant: we arrive at an understanding of the parts by studying the whole; but study of isolated parts will not lead to understanding of the whole.

The *yin-yang,* or "both-and," way of thinking enables us to understand the aspects of the Trinity in terms of the inclusive whole. This way of thinking presupposes the essential continuum in all things. In other words, *yin* and *yang* are different in existence but one in essence. Moreover, there is an essential continuum between the change and *yang* as well as between the change and *yin.* In the undifferentiated continuum of the divine nature the change (or the Creator) is *yin* (or the Spirit) in relation to *yang* (the Word). The change (or the Creator) is *yang* (or the Word) in relation to *yin* (or the Spirit). *Yin* (or the Spirit) is *yang* (or the Word) because both partake of the change (or the Creator). For the same reason *yang* (or the Word) is *yin* (or the Spirit). In this way we can perceive each aspect of the whole in relationship to the whole. *Yin-yang,* or "both-and" logic makes possible three in one and one in three. The three result from the existential differentiation of the divine into change (or the Creator), *yang* (or the Word), and *yin* (or the Spirit), but since essentially they are one undifferentiated continuum, they remain one. That one, which is the essential unity of divine nature, manifests itself as three different symbols. Thus it is oneness in three. The trinitarian formula is not *either* threeness in one *or* oneness in three; it is *both* threeness in one *and* oneness in three.

The trinitarian formula of "oneness in three and threeness in one" is the perfect symbol of divine nature. It symbolizes the inner process of change itself. In other words, it is the archetypal symbol of changing process, which is the basis of all changing phenomena. "One" represents the absolute unity of divine nature, while "three" represents the manifestations of divine nature in the world. Divine creativity proceeds from unity to diversification: "Tao produced the one. The one produced the two. The two produced the three. And the three produced the ten thousand things."[26] In the *Tao te ching, tao* represents godhead, the background and creative forces of the creator. The three (three lines, or trigrams) form the basic unit of everything in the world. The trigrams represent the all-embracing character of ultimate reality. It is the symbolic number of the many, which is the differentiation of the one.

The process of change consists of the movement from unity to diversity, or from one to many. Thus the divine movement from one to three, that is, the movement from unity to diversity, is the archetype of the changing process. Creation is the external manifestation of inner movement in the trinitarian life of God. The creation story in the Old Testament is the story of diversification: the separation of heaven from earth, light from darkness, water from dry land, and so forth. In the Upanishads this idea is more explicitly expressed: "It [Brahman] thought: 'May I be many; may I grow forth.' It created fire. That fire thought: 'May I be many; may I grow forth.' It created water. That is why, whenever a person is hot and perspires, water is produced from fire alone."[27] This divine movement from unity to diversity, or from single to many, is the inner process of change. This movement from the single to the many, or from one to three, is the process of growth.

On the other hand the inner movement of the divine from the many to the single, or from the three to the one, is the process of contraction. Just as the changing process consists of expansion and contraction, the trinitarian life of God is constantly in process of expansion and contraction. This divine process is the archetype of all changing process in the world. In this respect, the creative process of this world is merely the reflection of the inner life of the trinitarian God. In other words, what is happening in this world of change and transformation has already taken place in eternity. It is the divine movement from the one to the three and from the three to the one that makes everything change in the world.

The movement from the one to three, or from the single to the many, is the process of dividing, and the movement from three to one, or from the many to the single, is the process of uniting. The primordial mode of change is then the process of dividing and uniting. To change means to divide the united and to unite the divided. To divide the united means to transform from *yang* (——) to *yin* (— —), and to unite the divided means to transform from *yin* (— —) to *yang* (——). The primordial process of change is the constant mutual transformation of *yin* and *yang*, since everything is of *yin* and *yang*. By transforming *yin* to *yang* (or uniting the divided) and *yang* to *yin* (or dividing the united), all things change. Therefore the trinitarian activity of God, that is, eternal movement from unity to diversity and from diversity to unity, is the foundation of all changing process. The trinitarian formula is thus the perfect symbol of inner change and the primordial unit of creative process in the world.

The movement from the single to the many and the movement from the many to the single are mutually interdependent. The former creates multiple manifestations and the latter a single reality, each of which is an aspect of the other—in other words, "one in three and three in one." The relationship between single reality and multiple manifestations was well illustrated by Fa-tsang, a Chinese Buddhist monk. He describes arranging eight mirrors, facing inward, symmetrically around the perimeter of a circle, with two more mirrors, facing each other, above and below the center of the circle. In the center he placed a Buddha image. Each mirror reflected the Buddha image, and each mirror's image was reflected in the other mirrors. Multiplicity in unity and unity in multiplicity—or three in one and one in three—are possible because unity and multiplicity are *essentially* undifferentiated.

To understand the trinitarian formula in terms of essential continuum and existential differentiations accords with the primary intention of the early church fathers, that is, to see God as the essentially undifferentiated one and the existentially differentiated three. It is, therefore, not the doctrine itself but the Aristotelian interpretation of it that creates problems in understanding. Using *yin-yang,* or "both-and," logic threeness in one and oneness in three are seen to be reality, free of mystery or paradox. The *yin-yang* way of thinking, based on essential monism and existential dualism as set forth in the *I ching,* is in harmony not only with the Judeo-Christian worldview but with the twentieth-century concept of the relative and changing world. Thus it can be a most useful instrument of Christian faith.

Notes

1. Edmund Jacob, *Theology of the Old Testament* (New York: Harper and Brothers, 1958), p. 121.

2. See Wm. Theodore De Bary, ed., *Sources of Indian Tradition* (New York: Columbia University Press, 1958), 1:75, n. 10.

3. J. Y. Lee, *The I: A Christian Concept of Man* (New York: Philosophical Library, 1971), pp. 77ff.

4. Jacob, *Theology of the Old Testament*, p. 124.

5. *The Bhagavad Gita*, trans. Franklin Edgerton (Cambridge: Harvard University Press, 1972), xiv, 3.

6. Ibid., p. 152.

7. Ibid., vii, 4, 5.

8. The Heart Sutra, 10: "Form is emptiness and the very emptiness is form." Here "form" (*rūpa*) signifies the material or physical aspect of the world, while "emptiness" (*śūnyatā*) signifies the invisible, or spiritual, nature that is the counterpart of *rūpa*. See Edward Conze, trans., *Buddhist Wisdom Books* (London: George Allen and Unwin, 1958), pp. 80ff.

9. *Kaushitaki Upanishad*, III, 2, in *The Thirteen Principal Upanishads*, trans. Robert E. Hume, 2nd ed. (London: Oxford University Press, 1931), pp. 321f.

10. *Brihad-Āranyaka Upanishad*, IV, i, 3, in ibid., p. 128.

11. Paul Tillich, *Systematic Theology* (Chicago: University of Chicago Press, 1963), 3:21.

12. Anagarika Govinda, *Foundations of Tibetan Mysticism* (New York: Samuel Weiser, 1969), p. 152.

13. Ibid., p. 151.

14. Tillich, *Systematic Theology*, 3:162ff.

15. Tillich realized that such a distinction might reintroduce a false dualism into theology. See ibid., p. 113.

16. Anagarika Govinda, *Foundations of Tibetan Mysticism*, p. 138.

17. Emil Brunner, *The Christian Doctrine of God* (Philadelphia: Westminster Press, 1950), p. 30.

18. *Brihad-Āranyaka Upanishad*, II, iv, 14; III, iv, 2, in *Thirteen Principal Upanishads*, pp. 101–2, 112.

19. The spirit is analogous to a woman who is head of a family. As a woman, she is *yin*, but as family head, she is *yang*. In like fashion the Son, or Word, which is essentially *yang* in relation to the spirit, becomes *yin* in relation to the Father. Since *yin* and *yang* are essentially one and existentially differentiated, the spirit can act in its human manifestation as if it were *yang*.

20. Norman Pittenger, *God in Process* (London: SCM Press, 1967), p. 40.

21. *Tao te ching*, ch. 37, in *The Way of Lao Tzu*, trans. Wing-tsit Chan (New York: Bobbs-Merrill, 1963), p. 166.

22. Brunner, *Christian Doctrine of God,* pp. 205ff.
23. Tillich, *Systematic Theology,* 3:285.
24. Ibid.
25. Pittenger, *God in Process,* p. 40.
26. *Tao te ching,* 42.
27. *Chhāndogya Upanishad,* VI, ii, 2.

CHAPTER VII

FURTHER IMPLICATIONS
OF THE THEOLOGY OF CHANGE

The theology of change, as we have observed, presupposes a radical shift in our way of thinking and in our understanding God. It is based not on the substance of being but on the process of change, and change becomes the fundamental category of theological expression. This shift away from the substance of being to the process of change is based on a metaphysical principle expressed in the *I ching*. That principle is typically East Asian, but it is also compatible with our contemporary, relativistic worldview.

According to the theology of substance, being is prior to everything and change is therefore subordinate to being. In other words, change is a functional aspect of being. In the theology of change quite the reverse is true: it is not being that changes, but change that procreates the substance of being. In other words, change is not a mere function of being but the very source of becoming, the reality of being. Being is conceivable only because of becoming, and becoming is possible only because of change. Thus change is prior to all things.

As has been said in previous chapters, the theology of change repudiates the static and ontological symbols of God. The metaphysical symbol of God cannot be "being itself,"[1] because being is subsidiary to change. Since change is the basic category of description in the theology of change, the metaphysical symbol of God is "change itself," which is the source of all creativity. God as "change itself" transcends the changing world because "change itself" is constant, that is, changeless. But at the same time God as "change itself" is part of the changing world because "change itself" is the very source of all changing phenomena. The change that changes the world is known to us by its intrinsic and mutually complementary constituents of *yin* and *yang*. *Yin* always presupposes *yang*, and *yang* presupposes *yin*; neither could exist without the other. Therefore "both-and" logic is necessary to understand "change itself"; "either-or" logic, which is applicable to the category of being, is inapplicable to the category of change, in which conflict is not essential but existential. By use of the category of change and "both-and" logic I have attempted in previous chapters to correct the traditional Christian idea of God. Now let us turn our attention to some implications of the category of change for other problem areas of Christian faith.

THE FREEDOM OF HUMAN WILL

The apparent contradiction between free will and saving efficacy has in the past polarized Christian thinking into liberal and conservative or orthodox and unorthodox schools. The Pelagian controversy in the early fifth century almost forced Augustine to make a dogmatic assertion of humanity's original sin. The controversy between the Pelagian doctrine of free will and the Augustinian doctrine of original sin has recurred in many guises throughout the history of Christian thought. Sixteenth-century reformers reasserted the Augustinian doctrine of original sin and human depravity; the eighteenth and nineteenth centuries were almost completely dominated by the idea of free will; in the early twentieth century neo-orthodox thinkers strongly reasserted the Augustinian position. Responsible contemporary theologians are still plagued by the conflict between Augustine and Pelagius. But free will and original sin are perceived as irreconcilable opposites only because being is perceived as the ultimate category. If being is assumed to be the ultimate category, then free will *either* is *or* is not one of its endowments. Once again the concept of an ontic God entraps us in the "either-or" category of thinking. "Either-or" thinking permits no resolution of the age-old opposition between free will and original sin; it invites—in fact, requires—the dogmatic assertion and institutional enforcement of one position or the other, while the opposition between the ideas and the conflict between their adherents continues unabated.

The theology of change, however, regards the freedom of human will not as a substance or an endowment to be possessed, but as a process of change or an inclination to change toward fuller self-realization. In other words, human free will is not a static entity or substance of being which gives the direction of movement but is the power of inclination inherent in the process of self-realization.

This becomes clear to us if we define original sin, which became the converse or counterpart of free will in the history of Christian thought. Original sin is not a substance of being but the power of disinclination to harmonize oneself with the process of change. In other words, original sin is an inclination to oppose the self to the process of change, while free will is a spontaneous inclination to harmonize the self with the process of change. But the power of *both* harmonious *and* disharmonious inclinations is inherent in all things. Therefore humanity is free and bound by sin. We cannot say that we are *either* free *or* bound, because we are simultaneously free *and* bound. That is the real meaning of the famous paradox, *simul iustus et peccator.*

NATURAL THEOLOGY IN THE CHRISTIAN FAITH

As the authority of scholasticism waned, natural theology became a dominating theological issue. Franciscan scholars such as John Duns Scotus (1265–1308) and William of Occam (1300?–?1349) attacked the realism of Aquinas, and their arguments became seminal to and were reinforced by the Protestant Reformation. The breakdown of the Thomistic synthesis marked the beginning of real struggle between proponents of natural and of revealed theology. The Protestant traditions of *sola scriptura* and *sola fide* have seriously undermined natural theology in the Christian faith. The contemporary opposition between natural and revealed theology dates from Kierkegaard's counterattack against Hegelian metaphysics. Against Hegelian objectivism Kierkegaard asserts subjectivity through faith and dismisses objective reality. Barth restates Kierkegaard's opposition to natural theology in his first book, *The Epistle to the Romans*, and later writes, "I am an avowed opponent of all natural theology."[2] Following Barth, growing numbers of theologians in the past decade have rejected natural theology. Perhaps the most sensational debate on natural theology occurs in Barth's "No!," written in response to Emil Brunner.[3] Brunner allows *theologia naturalis* but reduces it to insignificance: God reveals himself in creation, but humanity, by reason of sin, is unable to perceive the revelation.[4] In North America, on the other hand, there has been a steady growth of natural theology among followers of such men as Henry Nelson Wieman and Alfred North Whitehead, who for their part dismiss the importance of revealed theology.

Natural theology was important in the Thomistic synthesis. The natural knowledge of God was demonstrated by the so-called cosmological argument, which was further developed by Anselm in his famous ontological proof of God. But though natural theology became an important part of epistemology, it never became important in soteriology. Following Reformation tradition, most theologians in recent decades have failed to define natural theology's proper place in God's saving work. Humanity can understand God through reason but cannot be saved by reason. Therefore natural theology is almost completely eliminated from soteriology. Any theology, however, that dismisses either the natural or the revealed knowledge of God is imbalanced and inadequate.

What is the response of the theology of change to the problem of natural theology? According to the theology of change, God's redemptive and creative work are *essentially* one and inseparable. Their distinctions are only existential. In other words, as I have pointed out, salvation is a process of God's creativity. Thus there is no absolute distinction between natural and revealed theology. Natural theology is essential for revealed theology, just as creation is essential for salvation. Their relationship is comparable to that of *yin* and *yang*. Just as *yin* is necessary for *yang*, revealed theology is necessary for natural theology. Just as the Creator and

Savior are inseparable, natural theology is inseparable from the process of salvation. Both natural and revealed theology are mutually inclusive and complementary in all aspects of the Christian faith. This complementary relationship between revealed and natural theology is important not only to ecumenism but to the ecological import of the Christian faith.

THE WRATH OF GOD IN THEOLOGY

The problem of reconciling God's wrath with God's love became a theological issue as early as the second century. Marcion's endeavor to differentiate between the wrathful God of the Old Testament and the loving God of the New Testament had failed to solve the problem. A serious attempt to solve this problem is apparent in the work of Luther, who called God's wrath the "strange work," "*opus alienum.*" It is alien to God because it does not come from God's essential will. Emil Brunner and Gustaf Wingren, among others, seem to concur in Luther's idea.[5] On the other hand, Barth, Tillich, and others argue that divine wrath is subsumed in divine love.[6] Thus God's wrath is either dismissed as "strange," not belonging to God's proper office, or it is completely dissolved in God's love. The lack of theological interest in the idea of divine wrath is evident in almost all theological works. While God's love is exhaustively treated, God's wrath is almost completely neglected in theology.

But to call God's wrath "*opus alienum*" is in fact to deny that it is a genuine expression of divine will. On the other hand, to conceive God's wrath as merely one expression of his love is also unjust. To describe it, as Tillich does, as "the emotional symbol for the work of love,"[7] is to deny its uniqueness and the authenticity of its place in theology. Christian theology has been very one-sided, failing—or refusing—to recognize that the wholeness of divine activity includes both positive and negative attitudes of God toward humankind.

The theology of change, however, assigns God's wrath its proper place in Christian faith. Destruction is a necessary part of construction, and growth is not possible without decay. Without God's wrath there is no way for us to conceive of God's love.

Without judgment there can be no salvation. The love that does not presuppose its counterpart, wrath, is not a complete love. They are inseparable. God's love and wrath both belong to the very nature of God; they are of the essence of the changing process in terms of union and division or in terms of expansion and contraction. God's love moves toward the unity between the change and the changed. God's wrath divides them, so that the reunion can come again in the process of change. Both the uniting and the dividing are the ways of change, the primordial activities of *yin* and *yang*. When *yang* (———) is divided, it becomes *yin* (— —). When *yin* is united, it becomes *yang*. Thus the essence of change is the movement of two primordial processes: the division of the united and the union of the divided, that is, God's wrath and God's love.

GOD'S PASSIBILITY

One of Christianity's most neglected doctrines is that of divine passibility, or capacity for suffering. About half a century ago Mozley pointed this out and concluded that God in fact ought to be impassible.[8] More recently Tillich writes that present-day theology tries to avoid the issue of divine passibility "either by ignoring it or by calling it an inscrutable divine mystery."[9] "But such escape," he continues, "is impossible in view of the question's significance for the most existential problem of theodicy. . . . If theology refuses to answer such existential questions, it has neglected its task."[10] Nevertheless, despite his own insight, Tillich's *Systematic Theology* devotes only two of its nearly thousand pages to God's passibility.[11]

The doctrine of divine impassibility was born of the church's struggle against the Patripassian "heresy." Patripassianism, as the word itself indicates, asserts the co-suffering of the Father with the Son. But if, as the church maintained, God is unchanging, then God the Father cannot suffer, since suffering—indeed, any emotion—predicates the ability to change in response to stimuli. Aquinas himself was led by his use of Aristotelian ontology to conclude that God is impassible. Clearly the traditional doctrine of divine impassibility was based on the traditional doctrine of static ontology, which became the basic theological category. Since God was thought to be unchanging being, passibility, which is emotional change, cannot be attributed to him.

The theology of change presupposes that reality is changing. What is real is changing, and what is not real is unchanging. Since God is the "change itself," he must be passible. Moreover, he is the source of all possibility and change. The theology of change completely reverses the attributes of divinity based on the theology of being. Furthermore, the idea of a passible God accords with the interdependence of *yin* and *yang*. Below is the map of the Great Ultimate (*Tai chi t'u*), which is the metaphysical symbol of change:

There is *yang* (the light dot) in *yin* (the dark area) and *yin* (the dark dot) in *yang* (the light area). This mutually inclusive relationship is a pictorial expression of Jesus' words: "I am in the Father and the Father in me." Because of the empathic and mutually inclusive relationship between the Father and the Son, the Son's suffering cannot but be also the Father's. Thus the theology of change can help us to understand the idea of divine passibility, which is, as Tillich said, urgently needed in our theology.

THE RESURRECTION OF THE DEAD

I have briefly discussed the meaning of resurrection in relation to crucifixion in the fifth chapter, but since the concept of resurrection is not only the seal of faith but the hope of believers, we must understand what is involved in believing in the resurrection of the dead. Jesus' resurrection is the central affirmation of Christian faith, in contemporary no less than in traditional theology. Bultmann, for example, stresses the existential meaning of resurrection and dismisses almost completely the significance of its historical reality. Wolfhart Pannenberg, on the other hand, asserts that the historical reality of Christ's resurrection is the key to the understanding of Christology.[12] At issue between these two interpretations is the hermeneutic definition of the reality of resurrection and the more fundamental question of the renewal of life in a new, or spiritual, body. In other words, "for Paul, resurrection means the new life of a new body."[13] The resurrection of the dead is quite different from the immortality of the soul.

Paul tried very hard to make the Corinthians understand the idea of a new, or spiritual body, but it is questionable whether they understood him. As Cullmann said, "An incorruptible body! How are we to conceive this?"[14] The theology of substance cannot deal with such an idea. Therefore let us turn to the theology of change.

The hermeneutic conflict between the existential and the historical definitions of resurrection needs to be resolved. The former stresses the subjective experience of resurrection, the latter the objective historical reality of resurrection. According to the category of being, that is, the "either-or" way of thinking, there is no way to resolve the conflict between subjective and objective reality. But according to the category of change, that is, the "both-and" way of thinking, subjective and objective reality are mutually inclusive and complementary. In the world of constant change and transformation a historical fact is only real to us if it is part of our experience.

The idea of a spiritual, or incorruptible, body is virtually inconceivable in "either-or" terms because body is by definition corruptible and spirit is by definition incorruptible, and in the "either-or" way of thinking the one must exclude the other. But the theology of change, which employs the "both-and" way of thinking, can help us conceive of an incorruptible body. According to the metaphysics of change everything is simultaneously both *yin* and *yang*. Just as *yin* is in *yang* and *yang* is in *yin*, the spiritual body and the physical body are each part of the other. That may be what Paul means by saying, "If there is a physical body, there is also a spiritual body" (1 Cor. 15:44). A new discovery has been made concerning the coexistence of the physical and spiritual body: "In 1968, Doctors V. Inyushin, V. Grishchenko, N. Vovoben, N. Shouiski, N. Fedorova and F. Gibadulin announced their discovery: All living things—plants, animals, and humans—not only have a physical body made of atoms and molecules, *but also a counterpart body of energy*: They called it 'the Biological Plasma Body.' "[15] Whether we call the counterpart of the physical body the Biological Plasma Body or the spiritual body, it seems to exist in all physical bodies. At the time of death the physical body disintegrates and is reduced to its minimum and the spiritual body expands to its maximum. Therefore, we can conceive the life of the other side in the spiritual body because of the life of this side in the physical body. It is then possible for us to understand what Paul means when he speaks of the coexistence of the spiritual and the physical bodies.

The theology of change also suggests the possibility of reincarnation, which is not the same as resurrection. According to the principle of change, anything that has reached its minimum begins to expand toward its maximum. The physical body, which is reduced to its minimum at death begins to expand again toward its maximum, while the spiritual body, which is at its maximum at death begins to contract again. This expanding process of the physical body, that is, the process of reincarnation, has been slighted by traditional theology.[16]

THE IDEA OF *ESCHATON*

The growing contemporary interest in the theology of hope has brought eschatology to the forefront of theology. Bultmann's dictum that Christ's eschatological presence is known existentially has been almost completely replaced by hope in a future *eschaton*. In other words, the existential encounter with Christ is no longer the key element of the kingdom of God. Rather, the theology of hope makes hope the focus of the whole of history, and the end of time the ultimate dimension of time. The end of time, according to the theology of hope, confers authenticity on both past and present.

The question of the end of time raises many theological issues, as Brunner points out.[17] I wish to discuss only whether the *eschaton* can be the ultimate dimension of time. In terms of the theology of change can the future be the ultimate upon which past and present are contingent?

According to the theology of change the end always presupposes the beginning. End and beginning are inseparable, like *yin* and *yang*. Therefore the end cannot be the ultimate dimension of time. But neither can there be an independently existing present. In other words, in the world of change there is no independently existing moment of "now." There are only two dimensions of time, the future and the past, and the present is always both the future and the past. A present moment independent of the future and the past is an illusion of being. To exist means to be in both the future and the past. Therefore the future cannot be absolutized. We cannot say that the past is totally dependent on the future, because the future is also dependent on the past. Authentic time is *both* future *and* past. Therefore the *eschaton* cannot become the ultimate dimension of time.

In the theology of change time does not exist by itself, independent of change. It is not time that changes the world but the change that changes time. Time is the unit of changing process, the measurement of change. Thus time moves always in the pattern of change. Since change is essentially a process of expansion and contraction, time also moves between the past and the future or the end and the beginning. Just as the minimum of *yin* is the maximum of *yang*, the end of the old is the beginning of the new. The world constantly renews itself, so that the end of the old world is also the beginning of the new, because God is the source of renewal and change. Thus the *eschaton* is both the end of the old time and the beginning of the new time.

I have attempted to demonstrate how the theology of change can illuminate some problem areas of Christian faith. Most problems in theology originated in the ontological, or "either-or," framework of traditional Christianity. This ontological framework, in which being is assumed to be absolute, was itself based on the static worldview that has been disproved by contemporary scientific development. The theology of change employs the relative, or "both-and," category of thinking, which is compatible with the world of relativity. A fully developed theology of change might therefore be able to reconcile the differences between science and religion as well as between East and West.

Notes

1. See Chapter 3.
2. Karl Barth, *The Knowledge of God and the Service of God* (London: Hodder and Stoughton, 1938), p. 6.
3. Barth's "No!" and Brunner's "Nature and Grace" are found in John Baille, ed., *Natural Theology*, trans. Peter Fraenkel (Geoffrey Bles, Ltd.; The Centenary Press in London, 1964).
4. E. Brunner, *The Christian Doctrine of God* (Philadelphia: Westminster Press, 1950), pp. 132ff.
5. See Gustaf Wingren, *Gospel and Church*, trans. Ross Mackenzie (Philadelphia: Fortress Press, 1964), p. 98; Brunner, *Christian Doctrine of God*, pp. 230ff.
6. Karl Barth, *Church Dogmatics*, II/1 (Edinburgh: T. & T. Clark, 1956), 362ff; P. Tillich, *Systematic Theology* (Chicago: University of Chicago Press, 1951), 1:183ff.
7. Tillich, *Systematic Theology*, 1:284.
8. J. K. Mozley, *The Impassibility of God* (Cambridge: Cambridge University Press, 1926), p. 128.
9. Tillich, *Systematic Theology*, 3:404.
10. Ibid.
11. Kenneth Woollcombe, "The Pain of God," *Scottish Journal of Theology* 20, no. 2 (June 1967): 132.
12. W. Pannenberg, *Jesus: God and Man*, trans. Lewis Wilkins and D. A. Priebe (Philadelphia: Westminster Press, 1968), pp. 88ff.
13. Ibid., p. 75.
14. Oscar Cullmann, *The Immortality of the Soul or Resurrection of the Dead* (London: Epworth, 1958), p. 40.
15. Shelia Ostrander and Lynn Schroeder, *Psychic Discoveries Behind the Iron Curtain* (Englewood Cliffs: Prentice-Hall, 1970), p. 213.

16. The idea of reincarnation is dismissed by most theologians as irrelevant to the Christian faith. Weatherhead, however, considers the doctrine of reincarnation in a Christian context. He says, "Now to be serious, can Christians believe in reincarnation? I think they can. That is to say, I don't see anything in this theory which contradicts the Christian position. In our Lord's time it was part of the accepted beliefs of everybody. Indeed, it was accepted by the Christian until 553 when the Council of Constantinople rejected it by a very narrow majority." See Leslie D. Weatherhead, *Life Begins at Death* (Nashville and New York: Abingdon Press, 1969), p. 71.

17. See E. Brunner, *Eternal Hope*, trans. by H. Knight (Philadelphia: Westminster Press, 1954), pp. 114ff.

INDEX

INDEX

Abraham, 31
absolute theology, 19,20
acosmism, 71
actualization, 15
Adam, 59
agape, 71
Ahriman, 66n
ākāsa (sense-organs), 82
America, and theology, 12
Analects, 9n
analogy of being, as Anti-Christ, 12
analogy of relation, 12,85n
analytic method, 17
androgyny, 51
angels, 24
Anselm, 123
anti-Christ, 12
apocalyptic writers, and cosmic dualism, 58
apocalyptic writings, 57
Aquinas, Thomas, 11,29,30,68
    and divine impassibility, 125–26
    and doctrine of analogy, 84n
    and natural theology, 122–23
archaic pictogram "chameleon," 2
archetype, of humanity, 100,111
Arian "heresy," 86
Aristotelian logic, 59
    and western science, 16
Aristotelian metaphysics, 25–26,29
Aristotelian philosophy, fundamental
    category of, 12
Aristotelianism, 11
Asia Minor, 102n
astronomy, and *I Ching*, 2
Athanasius, 86
Ātman, 45,56
    as individual self, 76
    as spirit, 108
atoms
    and hexagrams, 8
    and metaphysics, 79–80
Attis, 102n

Augustine, 11,29,68
    on original sin, 72,121
Aulén, 58

Babylon, 102n
Babylonian cult, 57
Barth, Karl, 12,23,32,68
    on the covenant, 73–74
    on definition of Christ, 93
    on divine wrath, 124
    on divinity and humanity, 72
    on natural theology, 123
    on the Trinity, 111–12
Bartsch, Werner, 28n
becoming, 36,38,42
    in Hebrew thought, 19
    process of, 16,18,69
being, 36
    in Greek thought, 19
"being itself," as subsidiary to change,
    120–21
Berdyaev, Nicholas, 70
Bhagavad Gita, 105
Bible, 67
"biological plasma body," 128
biology, and changing universe, 23
Boman, Thorleif, 19,27n,36
Bonhoeffer, Dietrich, 68,71,77
    on Adam and good and evil, 59
    on transcendence, 49
Book of Changes, see *I Ching*
"both-and," 17–20
    as category of ultimate reality, 49
    and contemporary theology, 64
    and divine nature in Judeo-Christian
        teachings, 50
    and the *eschaton*, 129–30
    and God, 18
    and God's attributes, 49
    and spiritual and physical bodies,
        127–28
    and the Trinity, 114–17
    and *yin-yang*, 20

135

Brahman, 32–33,45
  as the cosmic self, 76
  as creator God, 67
  as neuter pronoun *it*, 52
  and spirit and matter, 104–6
  as true self of cosmos, 56
Brahman/Ātman synthesis, 56
breath, *see* spirit
Brihad-Aranyaka Upanishad, 65n, 118n
British Anthropological Society, 2
broken line, *see yin*
Brunner, Emil, 88,91–92
  on divine wrath, 124
  on eschaton, 129
  on Trinity, 112
Buddha, 71
Buddhism, 26,69,
  supreme reality in, 33
Bultmann, Rudolf, 12,23–24,58,68
  on resurrection, 127
  on Trinity, 112
burning bush, 54, 76
Butterworth, Eric, 85n

Callistus, 29
Calvin, John, 11,68
Calvinism, 72
Cartesian reform, 11
center
  as Christ, 97–98
  and spirit as inner essence, 109–10
  of trigrams, 55
Chalcedon, Council of, 86
Chameleon, as symbol of change, 2–3
Chang, Chung-Yuan, 15,27n,43
Chang Tsai, 77–78
Change, see also I
  and being and becoming, 18
  as beyond categorization, 22
  as "both-and" category, 18
  as creator, 78,80–84, 115
  and God's "is-ness," 42
  mechanism of, 5
  metaphysical meaning of, 3,21
  pattern of, 5
  as personal and impersonal reality, 22
  as transcendent and immanent, 22
  as ultimate reality, 15–16
change theology, *see* theology of change
"changing changer," 41
chen, the "awakening," 7

Chhāndogya Upanishad, 119n
Ch'ien, "heaven," 7,15,37,39,78
China, 1,2,26
  and concept of heaven, 37
  and cyclic time, 13
  and origin of *I Ching*, 9n
Chinese philosophy, 26
Chinese science, 2
Chinese trinity, 6,77–78
Chinese worldview, 105
ching, book or classic, 2
Chou dynasty, 9n
Chou Tun-i, 40
Christ, *see* Jesus Christ
Christocentric theology, 68
Christology, 86–101
  cosmic center in, 97–98
  the creation in, 89
  crucifixion and resurrection in, 100–01
  divinity and humanity in, 98–100
  Jesus, subordinate to Creator in, 88
  "the Light" in, 91–92
  problems of, 88
  Savior in, 92–97
  "the Word" in, 89–91
Christian church, 67
Christian faith
  and Hellenistic thinking, 1
  as metaphysical system, 25–26
  and modern science, 1
Christian message, as originally
    inclusive, 21
Christian mystics, 70–71
Christian theologians, 68
Christian theology
  and change, 25
  and ecology, 24–25
  foundation of, 11
  framework of, 26
  Greek influence on, 11
  wrath of God and, 1,24–25
Christianity
  and Asian religions, 1
  and ecumenism, 69
  exclusiveness of, 21,68
  philosophical modes in, 1
  as redemption-centered, 69
  uniqueness of, 21
  and world civilization, 1
chung kua, see hexagrams
Church Dogmatics (Karl Barth), 12

church fathers, 29
Chu'u Chai, 40
classical western worldview, 22
Cobb, John, 17,27n
conflict of good and evil, *see* theodicy
Confucian classics, 2
Confucius, 3,4,9n,46n,52
contemporary worldview, 22–23
"contrapetal" logic, 64
Conze, Edward, 70,84n
co-passion, doctrine of, 29
Corinthians, 127
cosmic center, 97–98
cosmic dualism, 57,63
cosmology
    eastern, 13
    western, 14
cosmos, 25
council
    of Chalcedon, 86
    of Constantinople, 131n
    of Nicea, 86
covenant, 73–76
creation, 69
    as a priori category of redemption, 68
    and covenant, 74–78
    as divine movement, 116
    "out of nothing," 70–71
    and salvation, 87–88
creative flux, 17
creative process, 13,15
creativity
    as basis of ecumenism, 69
    and the great *yang*, 15
    and heaven and earth interaction, 18
    process of, 15,39
    Syriac and Vulgate version of, 70
creator
    and creature, 71,72,73,–78
    as nonbeing, 70
crucifixion, 100–01
Cullmann, Oscar, 127
cult
    Babylonian, 57
    Persian, 57

dabhar, 89
Daniel, 57
death-of-God theology, 12
demonic power, 57–58
demons, in Synoptic Gospels, 58

Descartes, René, 30
deva-śakti images, 51
Devil, 61
Dewart, Leslie, 44
divination, in *I Ching*, 2
divine creativity, 68, 95
divine harmony, 111
divine movement, 116
divine nature, *see also* God
    in archaic religions, 51
    dipolarity of, 17
    as inclusive, 52
    in Judeo-Christian society, 51
divine passibility, 125–26
divine redemptivity, 68
divine wrath, 124–25
divinity and humanity, of Jesus, 98–100
doctrine
    of creation, 81
    of "creation out of nothing," 71–72
    of divine impassibility, 125–26
    of original sin, 72
    of salvation, 86–88
    trinitarian, 88
dragon, power of, 37
dualism, in Judeo-Christian expression, 57–58
dualistic logic, 18
dukkha, 92–93
duograms, 5–7
dynamic ontology, 12

early church, theology of, 88
earth
    characteristic of, 39
    in Chinese trinity, 6
    and idea of world, 18
    as mother, 77–78
    and second hexagram, 78
    and the great *yin*, 15
East, and organic worldview, 13,82
East Asia, 2
East Asian philosophy, and *I Ching*, 2
eastern church, 68
eastern cosmology, cyclic time of, 13
Ecclesiastes, 95
Eckhart, Meister, 25,34,45,64
ecological crisis, 24,28n
    as misunderstanding of divine nature, 54–55
    original cause of, 25

ecosystem, 1,24
    and change, 25
ecumenical council, *see* council
ecumenism, in East and West, 1,124
Egypt, 31,102n
ehyeh, 32
eight trigrams, *see* trigrams
eighth "wing," 10n
Einstein, Albert, 16,22,24
"either-or" logic, 16,60
    and free will, 121–22
    and God, 18
    and good and evil, 59
    and problem of Trinity, 113
    and spiritual and physical bodies,
        127–28
El, 37
Eleatic school, static worldview of, 16
electrons, 8,79
Eliade, Mircea, 51
elohim, 37,53
"emptiness," 45,91, *see also śūnyatā*
Enoch, 57
epistemology, and natural theology, 123
Epistle to the Hebrews, 43
Epistle to the Romans, The (Karl Barth), 123
epistles, cosmic powers in, 58
eschatology, 96,128
eschaton, 96,128–30
Euclidean geometry, 16,22
Euclidean worldview, 87
evil, as an existential problem, 59
"excluded middle," 113
existence
    nonpersonal, 25
    personal, 25
existential estrangement, 92–93
Exodus, Book of, 25,30–31,36
Ezra, 57

faith, *see* Christian faith, Judeo-Christian
        faith
Fall, of humanity, 59,72
Fa-tsang, 117
Ferré, Nels, 64
filial piety, and God and Jesus, 87–88
Ford, Kenneth, 85n
four images, 6,15,40
Fourth Gospel
    Christ as "the Light" in, 91–92
    the spirit of life in, 107
    the "Word" in, 90–91

free will, and original sin, 121–22
Fu Hsi, 9n
Fung Yu-lan, 40

Gebser, Jean, 27n
gender, of the divine nature, 50–52
Genesis
    Adam in, 59
    the creation in, 69,89,90
geometry, 16
    and the *I Ching*, 2
Germany, 12
Gnostic myths, 58,61
God
    Aristotelian notion of, 29,30
    and "both-and," 25
    as "change itself," 25
    as changeless change, 43–45
    contemporary ideas of, 12,24
    as creator, 88
    as creator and savior, 87–88
    doctrine of impassibility of, 29
    early names for, 31–32
    eastern nonsymbolic nature of, 32–35
    essence of being of, 12
    essence of change in, 30
    exclusive view of, 54
    as the Good, 19
    and good and evil, 57–64
    of Hebrews, 25
    and humanity, 72
    as impersonal, 25,50
    as inclusive and exclusive, 56
    as "is-ness itself," 32,35–36
    Judeo-Christian idea of, 30–32, 42, 51
    and logic, 25
    as "moving mover," 30
    as the nameless, 31–32
    nature of, consequent, 17
    as neglected creator, 67–68
    passibility of, 125–26
    as personal, 25,50
    as personal emancipator, 54
    and power, 37
    primordial idea of, 31–32
    primordial nature of, 17
    as source of creativity, 69–73
    symbols of, 30–32,120–21
    as totality of creative process, 18
    as transcendent and immanent,
        49,61,64
    as transcending "either-or" logic, 18

as ultimate and nonultimate, 71
as the "unmoved mover," 19
western nonsymbolic nature of, 30–32
and wind and breath of creation, 103–4,106–8
wrath and love of, 124–25
godhead, 25,70–71,74,110
gods, of destruction and preservation, 67
Good, the, 19
good and evil, *see* theodicy
Great Commentary, 3,5,7,15,18,39–40, 73,95–96
"Great Ultimate," 3,6,15,40,71,82
map of, 126
Greece, 89
Greek metaphysics, static ontology of, 13,29
Greek ontology, basis of, 11
Greek thought, basic category of, 19
Griffin, David, 27n
growth and decay, 23

harmony, of good and evil, 63
Harnack, Adolph, 11,26n
Hartshorne, Charles, 18,19,72
hayah, 31,36
Heart Sutra, 48n,106
heaven
  characteristic of, 39
  in Chinese trinity, 6
  as father, 77–78
  and first hexagram, 78
  and the great *yang*, 15
  and idea of God, 18
Hebrew thought, basic category of, 19
Hebrews
  concept of ultimate reality of, 37–38
  and the "Word," 89
  worldview of, 61,81–82
Hegelian essence, of dialectic process, 12
Hegelian metaphysics, 123
Heideggerian autonomy, 12
Heimann, Betty, 51,65n
hell, 24
Hellenistic philosophy, 11
Heremetica, 102n
hexagram
  compared with atom, 8
  and primal pattern of change, 8
  as *chung kua*, 6

and cyclic time, 13–14
diagram of formation of, 14
formation and arrangement of, 9n
as germinal units, 6,8
and interrelationships, 8
and subatomic particles, 79–80
as microcosmic symbol, 8,41
as double trigrams, 6,7
as "great trigrams," 7
Hinduism, 26,69
  and creator God, 67
  worldview of, 105
Hippolytus, 29
Holy Spirit, *see* Spirit
hope, theology of, 128–29
hot'u, see "river map"
Hsi-ming, 85n
Hsi tz'u, 41
hsiao sheng kua, see trigrams
humankind, and environment, 24,55,77

I, see also change
  as the chameleon, 2–3
  as Tao, 41
  as ultimate reality, 3,15
"I AM WHO I AM," 31–32,36
I Ching
  as ancient work, 2
  authorship of, 9n,47n
  and Chinese culture, 2
  and contemporary worldview, 8
  as Confucian classic, 9n
  cosmology of, 13
  and cyclic time, 96
  derivation of, 3
  and divination, 9n
  and duograms, trigrams, hexagrams, 5–9
  and East Asian philosophy, 1–2
  etymology of, 2–3
  and inclusive thinking, 18
  metaphysics of, 1–5,73,120–21
  monistic worldview of, 106
  philosophy of, 18
  as primordial ethos of East Asian peoples, 1–2
  and sixty-four hexagrams, 6
  and subatomic particles, 79–80
  and Taoism and Neo-Confucianism, 2
  theme of, 2
  and trinitarian structure of trigrams, 55

ultimate reality of, 15
as universe in microcosm, 8
as wisdom literature, 25
"I-It" relationship, 74–76
"I-Thou" relationship, 74–75
I t'ung, "explanation of change," 40
imago Dei, 77
im-mediated relationship, 74–76
"immovable first mover," 29
impassibility, doctrine of, 29
inclusive principle, 18
India, 13
inorganic forms, 23
intellection, as dualistic, 16–17
Irenaeus, 101n
Isaac, 31
Isaiah, 89
Islam, 69
"is-ness itself"
and concept of God, 32
dynamics of, 36–38
and nonsymbolic nature of God, 35–36
as Tao, 41
Israel, 31
and God's Word, 89
IT, Upanishadic symbol, 52

Jacob (O.T.), 31
Jacob, Edmund, 32
Japan, 1
Jeremiah, 89,109
Jesus Christ, *see also* Christology
as center of creative process, 97–98
as changeless, 43
crucifixion and resurrection of, 100–01
and darkness, 92
and the divine reality, 97–98
divinity and humanity of, 98–100
as the "light," 91–92
and salvation, 86–96
as savior, 68,92–97
as subordinate to creator, 88
symbolism of, 58,69,100
as true brother, 98
victory over evil of, 58,61
as the way of change, 93
as the "Word," 89–91
as *yang*, 92,94
John of the Cross, 97
John, prologue of, 102n
jou hsiao, see yin
Joyce, James, 20

Judaism, 69
Torah and wisdom in, 90
Judeo-Christian faith, *see also* Christian faith
core of, 67
as denying dualistic worldview, 81
worldview of, 61
Jung, Carl, 2,9n

kalpa, 13
k'an, 7
kang hsiao, see *yang*
Kantian categories, 12
Kantian synthetic forms, of categorical understanding, 12
Kaushitaki Upanishad, 118n
Ken, 7
Kierkegaard, Sören, 32
and divinity and humanity, 72
and natural theology, 122–23
Kierkegaardian realism, of subjectivity, 12
King Wen, 9n
koan, 62
Korea, 1
Ku Hung-ming, 52–53
k'un, 7,15,39,78, *see also* earth

Lao Tzu, 34,41,51,94
on creative process, 82
on the creator, 70
and notion of *Tao*, 53
on relativity of good and evil, 60
Last Judgment, 96
Lee, Jung Young
"Bultmann's Existentialist Interpretation and the Problem of Evil," 27n,28n,66n
Cosmic Religion, 85n
The I: A Christian Concept of Man, 28n, 85n,102n,118n
"Interpreting the Demonic Powers in Pauline Thought," 65n,66n
"Karl Barth's Use of Analogy in His Church Dogmatics," 27n,28n,84n
The Principle of Changes, 9n,10n,27n, 28n,48n,85n
"Some Reflection on Authorship of *I Ching*," 9n
"The Yin-Yang Way of Thinking," 9n,28n,102n
Leeuwen, Arend van, 36,37,53–54

Legge, James, 48n
leitmotiv
 of absolute theology, 20
 of change theology, 20
 of process theology, 20
li, 7
"life," as Tillich's ultimate reality, 15
lightning-thunder, primitive understanding of, 37
lines
 representing *yin-yang*, 4
 and "river map," 4
logic
 Aristotelian, 16
 "contrapetal," 64
 dualistic, 18
logogram, of "change," 2,3
logos, 34,37,53,89
love and wrath, of God, 124–25
Lundensian theology, 101n
Luther, Martin, 11,62,68,124

Mahayana Buddhism, 91,106
Malachi, 43,44
man
 and breath of life, 107
 as central line of trigram, 6
 in Chinese trinity, 6
 as product of *yin-yang*, 6
Marcion, 124
Margenau, Henry, 79
matter
 spatial and temporal element of, 16
 as spirit manifested, 104–6
māyā, 97–98,105
mechanistic worldview, 81
medicine, and *I Ching*, 2
meditation, and breathing, 107–8
Meland, Bernard, 27n
metaphysics, and *I Ching* cosmology,
 2–5,73
Michalson, Carl, 64
ming, 43
Moltmann, Jürgen, 75,101
monotheism, 108
moon, pictogram for, 3
moon cult, 37
morphogenesis, as symbol, 82–83
Moses, 30–31,35,76
Mount Meru, 97
Mount Sinai, 35
"moving mover," 30,41,75

Mozley, J.K., and divine impassibility,
 125–26
Munro, Donald, 45
Murray, John Courtney, 44
music, and *I Ching*, 2
mysterium logicum, 32
mystics, Christian, 70–71

Nagasena, 33–34
natural theology, 122–24
Nazi regime, 12
"neither-nor," 22,64
Neo-Confucianism, 2,77–78
neo-orthodox theology, 12
 and free will, 121
Neo-Platonism, 11,29
neo-Reformation theology, 12
Neotus, 29
neti, neti, 22,33,52,64
neutrons, 79
Neveille, Robert, 73
New Testament, 43
 cosmic dualism in, 63
 cosmology of, 23–24,61
 "demythologizing," 23
 end of the world in, 96
 good and evil in, 61
 loving God in, 124
 the Resurrection in, 101
 spirit of life in, 107–8
Newton, Isaac, and western logic, 16
Nicea, council of, 86
nihilism, 71
nihilo, 70
nirvana, 45
 as absolute nonexistence, 70
 etymology of, 33
 and matter and spirit, 106
Non-Ultimate, 71
North America, and natural theology, 123
nuclear physics, 22,24,25
 and change, 68
nuclei, 79
nucleus, of atom, 8

Ogden, Schubert, 27n,45,64
Ogletree, Thomas W., 48n
Old Testament, 31,37
 breath of life in, 107
 "life" and "light" in, 90
 monism of, 57
 wrathful God of, 124

"one," 115
ontic continuity, 72–78
ontology
    dynamic, 12
    static, 13
opus alienum, 124–25
Orient, 89
original sin
    doctrine of, 72
    and free will, 121–22
Ormazd, 66n
Osiris, 102n
Otto, Rudolf, 32

Pannenberg, Wolfhart, 68, 127
paradox, of Christian experience, 94
Patripassian "heresy," 29,125–26
Paul, 83–84,109
    Epistles of, and cosmic powers, 58
Pelagian controversy, 121
Pelagius, 121
Pentecost, 108
Persian cult, 57
Pharisees, 61
philosophy
    Aristotelian, 12
    Chinese, 26
    Eleatic, 19
    Greek, 13
    of Heidegger, 12
    Hellenistic, 11
    of *I Ching,* 18
    neo-Confucian, 77–78
    neo-Platonic, 29
    Platonic, 12,19
    Upanishadic, 56
physical body, and spiritual body,
    127–28
physics, 23,79,80
Pittenger, Norman, 13,27n,44,76,110
Planck, Max, 16
Plato, 2,12,19
    definition of God of, 36
Platonic metaphysics, 25–26
Platonic philosophy, 12
Platonic school, static worldview of, 16
pneuma, see Spirit
Po Chu-i, 34
power, primitive notion of, 37
prajñā, 91
Prajñāpāramitā-Sūtra, 45,91

Prāna, 103,107, *see also* Spirit
    as "mind," 82
Praxeas, 29
primordial ethos, of East Asian peoples,
    1–2
primordial matter, 105
problem of evil, 57–64, *see also* theodicy
"process," 15
process
    of becoming, 15,16
    and change, 15–16
    of creativity, 15
process theology, 24
    and American theology, 13
    and change theology, 13–20
    and character of the ultimate, 19
    and creativity, 20
    criticism of, 18
    as incomplete theology, 19–20
    and traditional theologies, 13
    as transitional theology, 19
    ultimate reality of, 15
    and western cosmology, 14
    worldview of, 13
"progress," 61
prophets, 43
Protestant Reformation, 122
protons, 79
"pure nothingness," 35
Purusha, "cosmic person," 82

quantum theory, 13,16

Radhakrishnan, S., 102n
Reason, and the "Word," 89
receptivity, the great *yin,* 15
redemption, 92
Reformers, 11
reincarnation, 128,131n
relativity, of good and evil, 62
relativity theory, 13,16,22,45,68
resurrection, 100–01
    of the dead, 126–28
    in Near Eastern beliefs, 102n
retrogression, 61
revealed theology, 122–24
Reverend Sariputta, 33
Richardson, Alan, 58
"river map," 3,9n
Roman Catholic theology, 11
ruach, see Spirit

rūpa, 118n
Russian myth, of God and Devil, 66n

Saher, P.J., 27n,28n
salvation, 86–88,92–97
samsara, 106
Samyutta-nikāya, 46n
Satan, 57–58
Savior, *see* Jesus Christ, Christology
Scharlemann, Robert P., 36
Schilling, Paul, 64, 66n
science
  Chinese, 2
  and process theology, 13
  western, 16
Scotus, John Duns, 122
Second Maccabees, on creation, 70
self-giving love, 71
Sermon on the Mount, 62
Shang Ti, "King of Kings," 53
Shao Yung, 14,82
Shintoism, 69
Shiva, 67,100
Shu, 45
Shuo Kua, eighth "wing," 10n
sin, 92–93
Sinai, 74
sixty-four hexagrams, *see* hexagrams
sive-sive, 52
Smith, Huston, 34
Smith, Wilfred C., 16,17,23,27n
sola fide, 122
sola scriptura, 122
solid line, *see* yang
Solomon, 55
sono-mama, 35,37–38
sophia, 90
soteriology, 68
  and natural theology, 123
soul, as Ātman 56
space age, 26
space and time, 16
spider, symbol of creator, 82
Spinoza, Benedict de, 38
Spirit, 103–17
  anonymity of, 110–11
  as archetype of humanity, 111
  as the breath of God, 109
  etymology of, 103–4
  as inner essence, 109–10
  as life and power, 106–8

  and matter, 104–6
  at Pentecost, 108
  as the power of change, 104
  and trinitarian doctrine, 88
  as *yin,* 110–11
spiritual body, 127–28
static concept, of being, 12
static ontology, 13
subatomic particles
  and change, 68
  and metaphysics, 79–80
substance
  Aristotelian notion of, 17
  concept of, 11
"suchness," 38
suffering, 92–93
  of the divine, 125–26
sun, 7
sun, pictogram for, 3
sun and moon, symbols of change, 3
Sung Neo-Confucianism, 40
Sūnyatā, 34,45,71,91
Suzuki, D.T., 35,41,45,91
Swami Prabhavananda, 45
symbol
  of Brahman, 97
  breath as, 108
  chameleon as, 2
  of cosmic center, 97
  of creative power, 90
  crucifixion and resurrection as, 100–01
  eight trigrams as, 7
  flying arrow as, 43
  of God, 30–32
  Jesus as "both-and" as, 100
  Jesus as, of creativity, 69
  Jesus' death as, 58
  light and life as, 91–92
  logos as, 53
  of masculine God, 51
  of the mediator, 99–100
  and morphogenesis, 82–83
  "moving mover" as, 75
  "one" as, 115
  of perfection (Taoism), 99
  of renewal, 96
  sixty-four hexagrams as, 41
  spider as, 82
  sun and moon as, 3
  "three" as, 115
  trigram and trinity as, 6

Trinity as, 111–14
and ultimate reality, 42
Upanishadic *IT* as, 52
waves and water as, 60
wind as, 104
Synoptic Gospels, demons in, 58
Systematic Theology (Paul Tillich), 15

Ta chuan, 3,9n,15,48n
ta sheng, 7, *see also* hexagrams
t'ai chi, 3,40,71
Tai chi t'u, 92
diagram of, 126
Takeda, Ryusei, 27n
Tammuz, 102n
Tao, 34
and anonymous spirit, 110
of Chinese Confucianism, 52
of Chinese Taoists, 53
of earth, 7–8
of heaven, 7
of man, 8
symbolized as "mother," 51
Tao te ching, 34,43,94,115
Taoism, 2,69
Taoist Scripture, 94

Tat tvam asi, "That thou art," 45, 76
temples, of creator God, 67
Ten commandments, 74
ten "wings," 9n
terra firma, 79
Tertullian, 29
theodicy, 50,57–64
theologians
and Aristotelian logic, 16
Christian, 68
contemporary, 77
theological thinking, three characteristic
forms of, 19
theology, *see also* Christian theology
of the absolute, 19
Christocentric, 68
creator-centered, 68–69
death-of-God, 12
of early church, 88
of ecology, 24
and "either-or" logic, 17
of fulfillment, 24
of hope, 12,128–29
Lundensian, 101n

natural vs. revealed, 122–24
neo-orthodox, 12
neo-Reformation, 12
process, 13–20
of substance, 120
task of, 23
traditional, 11–13
valid topics of, 1
western exclusive categories and, 16
and worldview, 24
theology of change
as acceptable Christian expression, 26
and "both-and" logic, 17–20
as creator-centered theology, 68–69
and divine passibility, 125–26
as ecumenical theology, 21–22
and the *eschaton*, 129–30
free will and original sin in, 122
as fundamental theology, 19
God's wrath in, 124–25
and inclusive principle, 18,20
logic in, 16–20
problem of natural theology in, 123–24
as rejecting dualism, 22
spiritual and physical bodies in,
127–28
as theology of fulfillment, 20
theory of relativity, *see* relativity theory
Thomistic synthesis, 122–23
three primal powers, 8
"three," 115
Til, Cornelius van, 12
Tillich, Paul, 12,15,25,27n,68
Christology in, 86
criticism of process theology of, 18
definition of Christ in, 92
definition of God in, 19,35,42
divine passibility in, 125–26
divine wrath in, 124
ontology of, 19
power of life in, 107–8
Trinity in, 112
time, *see also eschaton*
cyclic view of, 13, 96
different concepts of, 13–14
linear concept of, 13,87
and space, 16
Torah, as wisdom, 90
traditional theology, 11–13,80
transcendental viewpoint, 60
tres personae, 32,112

trigrams
  basic constituents of, 6
  as basic symbols, 6
  as basic units of universe, 6,7
  creation of, 6
  diagram of, 40
  as "small hexagrams," 7
  names of, 7
  origin of, 6
  as prototypes of hexagrams, 6
  trinitarian structure of, 55
  and *yin-yang* interaction, 6
trinitarian controversy, 68
trinitarian doctrine, 88
  problems of, 111–14
trinitarian dogma, 11
trinity
  in "both-and" logic, 114–17
  Chinese, 77–78
  doctrine of, 68
  and Nicea, 86
truth, as "both-and" category, 26
tui, 7
two primary forms, 15,40

ultimate reality, *see also* God, Tao, divine
    nature
  of *I Ching*, 15
  Confucian idea of, 52
  of process theology, 15
  symbols of, 42
  Taoist idea of, 52
  Tillich's "life" as, 15
  as transcending good and evil, 63
  as transcending subject and object, 17
una substantia, 32,112
unbroken line, *see* yang
unity, of God and the world, 17–18
universal process, 1
universe, as spirit manifested, 104–6
"unmoved mover," 19,30,44,75
Upanishads, 22,32,52,76
  the breathing spirit in, 106–8
  divine movement in, 116
  idea of God in, 56
Ushasta Cākrāyana, 56

Vedantic tradition, 105
Vedic literature, and "spirit" 103
Viṣhnu, 67

water, 60
"Way," the, 34,41
western cosmology, 14
western intellection, and "either-or"
    logic, 17
western philosophy, as footnotes to
    Plato, 2
western science, exclusive categories of,
    16
western theologians, and Aristotelian
    logic, 16
western theology, and exclusive cate-
    gories, 16
wheel, as analogy of change, 41
Whitehead, Alfred North, 2,12,14,15,
    17,19,27n,28n
  and the East, 38
  God and world in, 73
  natural theology of, 123
  organic worldview of, 24
Wieman, Henry Nelson, 123
Wilhelm, Hellmut, 28n
Wilhelm, Richard, 9n
William of Occam, 122
Williams, Daniel Day, 27n
wind, *see also* spirit,
  and power of God, 104,109
Wingren, Gustaf, 124
woman, analogous to spirit, 118n
"Word", the, 44,53,89–91,114
  and change, 83
  as wisdom of God, 90
world, as *yin*, 92
worldview
  dualistic Aristotelian, 16
  Chinese, 105
  classical western, 22
  contemporary, 16,22
  Euclidean, 87
  Hebrew, 61,81–82
  Hindu, 105
  Indian, 105
  Judeo-Christian, 61
  mechanistic, 81
  of New Testament, 23–24
  of process theology, 13
  relativistic, 60
  and theological inquiry, 23
  traditional eastern, 13,82
  classical western, 22
wu, "nothingness," 45

yah, 37
Yahweh, 37,44,53
Yājnavalkya, 56
yang, 14
  attributes of, 4
  as Christ, 92
  as the creative, 4
  function of, 94
  as "hard" line, 5
  as light principle, 3
  as the "Word," 115
YHWH, 31–32,33,35,36
yiheyh, 32
yin, 14
  attributes of, 4
  as dark principle, 3
  function of, 94
  as the receptive, 4
  as "soft" line, 5
  as the Spirit, 110–11,115
  as the world, 92
yin-yang
  as cardinal principles, 4,6,20
  and Christ's divinity and humanity,
    98–100
  as components of change, 4–5
  and creation, 78–80

  and crucifixion and resurrection,
    100–01
  and cyclic time, 14
  and the *eschaton*, 129–30
  as existential distinctions, 5
  explanation of, 3–5
  and God's love and wrath, 124–25
  and good and evil, 63
  as inclusive, 63
  and matter and spirit, 106
  as not duality, 4–5
  and ontic unity, 78–80
  and problem of trinity, 113–17
  prototypes of, 3
  as river map circles, 4
  and spiritual and physical bodies,
    127–28
  symbols of, 4
  and trigrams, 6
yin-yang school, 9n
yoga, and breath, 107–8

Zen *koan*, 62
Zen master, 62
Zoroastrianism, 58
  myth of good and evil in, 66n

Other Orbis books . . .

THE MEANING OF MISSION

José Comblin

"This very readable book has made me think, and I feel it will be useful for anyone dealing with their Christian role of mission and evangelism." *New Review of Books and Religion*

ISBN 0-88344-304-X CIP   *Cloth $6.95*

THE GOSPEL OF PEACE AND JUSTICE

Catholic Social Teaching Since Pope John

Presented by Joseph Gremillion

"Especially valuable as a resource. The book brings together 22 documents containing the developing social teaching of the church from *Mater et Magistra* to Pope Paul's 1975 *Peace Day Message on Reconciliation*. I watched the intellectual excitement of students who used Gremillion's book in a justice and peace course I taught last summer, as they discovered a body of teaching on the issues they had defined as relevant. To read Gremillion's overview and prospectus, a meaty introductory essay of some 140 pages, is to be guided through the sea of social teaching by a remarkably adept navigator."

National Catholic Reporter

"An authoritative guide and study aid for concerned Catholics and others." *Library Journal*

ISBN 0-88344-165-9   *Cloth $15.95*
ISBN 0-88344-166-7   *Paper $8.95*

THEOLOGY IN THE AMERICAS

Papers of the 1975 Detroit Conference

Edited by Sergio Torres and John Eagleson

"A pathbreaking book from and about a pathbreaking theological conference, *Theology in the Americas* makes a major contribution to ecumenical theology, Christian social ethics and liberation movements in dialogue." *Fellowship*

ISBN 0-88344-479-8 CIP   *Cloth $12.95*
ISBN 0-88344-476-3   *Paper $5.95*

LOVE AND STRUGGLE
IN MAO'S THOUGHT

Raymond L. Whitehead

"Mao's thoughts have forced Whitehead to reassess his own philosophy and to find himself more fully as a Christian. His well documented and meticulously expounded philosophy of Mao's love and struggle-thought might do as much for many a searching reader." *Prairie Messenger*

ISBN 0-88344-289-2 CIP   *Cloth $8.95*
ISBN 0-88344-290-6   *Paper $3.95*

WATERBUFFALO THEOLOGY

Kosuke Koyama

"This book with its vivid metaphors, fresh imagination and creative symbolism is a 'must' for anyone desiring to gain a glimpse into the Asian mind." *Evangelical Missions Quarterly*

ISBN 0-88344-702-9   *Paper $4.95*

ASIAN VOICES
IN CHRISTIAN THEOLOGY

Edited by Gerald H. Anderson

"A basic sourcebook for anyone interested in the state of Protestant theology in Asia today. I am aware of no other book in English that treats this matter more completely." *National Catholic Reporter*

ISBN 0-88344-017-2   *Cloth $15.00*
ISBN 0-88344-016-4   *Paper $7.95*

FAREWELL TO INNOCENCE

Allan Boesak

"This is an extremely helpful book. The treatment of the themes of power, liberation, and reconciliation is precise, original, and Biblically-rooted. Dr. Boesak has done much to advance the discussion, and no one who is interested in these matters can afford to ignore his important contribution." *Richard J. Mouw, Calvin College*

ISBN 0-88344-130-6 CIP   *Cloth $4.95*

THE CHURCH AND
THIRD WORLD REVOLUTION

Pierre Bigo

"Heavily documented, provocative yet reasonable, this is a testament, demanding but impressive." *Publishers Weekly*
ISBN 0-88344-071-7 CIP   *Cloth $8.95*
ISBN 0-88344-072-5   *Paper $4.95*

WHY IS THE THIRD WORLD POOR?

Piero Gheddo

"An excellent handbook on the Christian understanding of the development process. Gheddo looks at both the internal and external causes of underdevelopment and how Christians can involve themselves in helping the third world." *Provident Book Finder*
ISBN 0-88344-757-6   *Paper $4.95*

POLITICS AND SOCIETY
IN THE THIRD WORLD

Jean-Yves Calvez

"This frank treatment of economic and cultural problems in developing nations suggests the need for constant multiple attacks on the many fronts that produce problems in the human situation."
                                             The Christian Century
ISBN 0-88344-389-9   *Cloth $6.95*

A THEOLOGY OF LIBERATION

Gustavo Gutiérrez

"The movement's most influential text." *Time*
   "The most complete presentation thus far available to English readers of the provocative theology emerging from the Latin American Church." *Theological Studies*
   "North Americans as well as Latin Americans will find so many challenges and daring insights that they will, I suggest, rate this book one of the best of its kind ever written." *America*
ISBN 0-88344-477-1   *Cloth $7.95*
ISBN 0-88344-478-X   *Paper $4.95*

MARX AND THE BIBLE

José Miranda

"An inescapable book which raises more questions than it answers, which will satisfy few of us, but will not let us rest easily again. It is an attempt to utilize the best tradition of Scripture scholarship to understand the text when it is set in a context of human need and misery."

Walter Brueggemann, in Interpretation

ISBN 0-88344-306-6   *Cloth $8.95*
ISBN 0-88344-307-4   *Paper $4.95*

BEING AND THE MESSIAH

The Message of Saint John

José Miranda

"This book could become the catalyst of a new debate on the Fourth Gospel. Johannine scholarship will hotly debate the 'terrifyingly revolutionary thesis that this world of contempt and oppression can be changed into a world of complete selflessness and unrestricted mutual assistance.' Cast in the framework of an analysis of contemporary philosophy, the volume will prove a classic of Latin American theology." *Frederick Herzog, Duke University Divinity School*

ISBN 0-88344-027-X CIP   *Cloth $8.95*
ISBN 0-88344-028-8   *Paper $4.95*

THE GOSPEL IN SOLENTINAME

Ernesto Cardenal

"Upon reading this book, I want to do so many things—burn all my other books which at best seem like hay, soggy with mildew. I now know who (not what) is the church and how to celebrate church in the eucharist. The dialogues are intense, profound, radical. *The Gospel in Solentiname* calls us home."

Carroll Stuhlmueller, National Catholic Reporter

ISBN 0-88344-168-3   *Vol. 1 Cloth $6.95*
ISBN 0-88344-170-5   *Vol. 1 Paper $4.95*
ISBN 0-88344-167-5   *Vol. 2 Cloth $6.95*